Ian Jackson's
Animal
Portraits

Ian Jackson's
Animal
Portraits

Foreword by **Chris Packham**

Compiled by **Tig Thomas**

Contents

Snow and Ice

Family Life

Tooth and Claw

Fight or Flight

Foreword

by Chris Packham

The way that we think about other animal species has always been in a state of constant flux and will inevitably have an individual perspective. In this book, for example, Laurens van der Post revels in the roar of a lion that visits his bush camp, Charles Darwin remarks upon the satisfying snuffle made by a content tiger, and Ian Seraillier is excited by the visit of a wood mouse to his wainscoting. He is happier than I was not long ago when I arrived home to find that I too had entertained a mouse or two – they had chewed into and eaten several packets of crisps and all of my breakfast cereal! However, the roars of the Tsavo man-eaters were less welcome on the Kenyan railway, I imagine! And as much as we celebrate their beauty and cherish tigers as a conservation icon, if one ate your grandfather you might feel differently. Our inter-relationship can thus be fanciful, fraught, maybe even fickle, but as the many varied texts that accompany these exquisite portraits show, it is never short of fascinating. A highly eclectic and entertaining collection of essays, poems and comments are supported by some refreshing scientific observations, which are sure to teach old naturalists some new things – fish- and frog-eating leopards a case in my part. We can thus enjoy Ted Hughes' take on the wolf as the eternal hero/villain, experience nostalgia as Gilbert White describes the delightful harvest mouse as a new species, and delve into the contemporary diaries of Sir David Attenborough to discover that the redder an uakari monkey's face, the more resistant it is to malaria. But of course this is only half the celebration on offer.

Ian Jackson's meticulous portraits are superb feats of photo realism; every whisker and each hair is precisely drawn but never at the expense of the actual character of the creature displayed – the pictures are greater than the sum of their highly detailed parts. Many of the animals portrayed are 'in action' so many are set in their natural environments, and it is clear that Ian's artistic invention shows no leaning to the easiest option. It's difficult to single out favourites, but for me the sloth bears and pine marten are fabulous, and the gruesome false vampire bat is… delicious!

The rest of the world's species do not live in isolation from us. Indeed, an increasing number are becoming dependent upon human intervention for their survival. We need to choose to protect them and we cannot rise to this challenge unless we have as many people on board as possible. I hope you may consider using some of the joy you derive from this book to motivate some active conservation. Whatever you do, share these pages with your children or grandchildren – the world they are set to inherit will need even more dedication to ensure it continues to thrive.

7

Great and Small

BROWN BEAR

from 'Evangeline'
by Henry Wadsworth Longfellow

Here and there rise groves from the margins of swift-running rivers;
And the grim, taciturn bear, the anchorite monk of the desert,
Climbs down their dark ravines to dig for roots by the brook-side...

Like all bears, brown bears have a large snout and keen sense of smell. However, their sight and hearing are less well developed and they have small eyes and ears.

Scientific name	*Ursus arctos*
Distribution	Northern Europe, Siberia, Asia, Alaska, Canada, mountainous areas of western USA
Habitat	Forest, tundra
Size	Body: 1.5–2.5 metres
Status	Least Concern

MANDRILL

from *The Life of Mammals*
by Sir David Attenborough

A scarlet streak runs from between his eyes down to the tip of his nose. There it broadens to cover nostrils and his upper lip. On either side of his nose, he has ridges of naked skin that is electric blue. The grooves between them are purple. This extraordinary face is surrounded by a band of white fur with above a brown crest and below an orange beard. Such astounding, extravagant faces go far beyond what is required to identify an animals' species.

Male mandrills bare their enormous fangs when they are anxious or want to scare other males. The fangs may reach up to 7 centimetres in length.

Scientific name	*Mandrillus sphinx*
Distribution	Africa
Habitat	Forest
Size	Body: 55–95 centimetres
Status	Vulnerable

FALLOW DEER

from 'The Deer's Request'
by Elizabeth Jennings

We are the disappearers.
You may never see us, never,
But if you make your way through a forest
Stepping lightly and gently,
Not plucking or touching or hurting,
You may one day see a shadow
And after the shadow a patch
Of speckled fawn, a glint
Of a horn.
Those signs mean us.

O chase us never. Don't hurt us.
We who are the male carry antlers
Horny, tough, like trees,
But we are terrified creatures,
Are quick to move, are nervous
Of the flutter of birds, of the quietest
Footfall, are frightened of every noise.

Male fallow deer have large, broad, flat antlers. They can become very aggressive during the mating season and they fight one another to get more does, or females, in their group.

Scientific name	*Dama dama*
Distribution	Europe
Habitat	Woodlands
Size	85–100 centimetres to the shoulder
Status	Least Concern

COMMON WASP

from *Fabre's Book of Insects*
by Jean-Henri Fabre

The wasp's nest is made of a thin, flexible material like brown paper, formed of particles of wood. It is streaked with bands, of which the colour varies according to the wood used. If it were made in a single continuous sheet it would give little protection against the cold. But the Common Wasp, like the balloon-maker, knows that heat may be preserved by means of a cushion of air contained by several wrappers. So she makes her paper-pulp into broad scales which overlap loosely and are laid on in numerous layers. The whole forms a coarse blanket, thick and spongy in texture and well filled with stagnant air. The temperature under this shelter must be truly tropical in hot weather…the wasp, then, often acts in accordance with the laws of physics and geometry. She employs air, a non-conductor of heat, to keep her home warm; she made blankets before man thought of it; she builds the outer walls of her nest in the shape that gives her the largest amount of room in the smallest wrapper; and in the form of her cell, too, she economises space and material.

These widespread insects build their football-sized nests underground or in buildings. There can be up to 6000 wasps in a colony. They feed on other insects but will also eat fruit, and they have been known to steal honey from bees' nests.

Scientific name	*Vespula vulgaris*
Distribution	Much of the Northern Hemisphere and introduced to Australia and New Zealand
Habitat	Gardens, woodlands
Size	Body: 10–14 millimetres
Status	Least Concern

JAGUAR

from 'Inspiration'
by Stuart Dybek

To the flowers
Come all manner of butterflies
And newly invented species of small
Colorful birds, twining serpents
And deep in the shadows
The mascaraed black-slit golden eyes
Of what may have been a jaguar.

*The jaguar is a good swimmer and likes to hunt
around rivers, lakes and swamps. It catches water
creatures such as turtles, crayfish and snakes,
as well as deer, monkeys and birds.*

Scientific name	*Panthera onca*
Distribution	Southwest USA, northern Mexico, Central and South America to northern Argentina
Habitat	Swampy rainforest, grassland
Size	1.6–2.5 metres including tail
Status	Near Threatened

Illustrator's note

"Of all the wildlife subjects I work on, my
absolute favourites are mammals, particularly
the large animals. Reflections are not
something you can usually find specific
references for, so this is one area where I
have to use my imagination."

14

KOMODO DRAGON

from *The Living Planet*
by Sir David Attenborough

When you see dragons gathered around a carcass, their potential ferocity and strength becomes more apparent. A large one is fully able to pick up a goat's carcass with its jaws and drag it boldly away. If two large ones are feeding on it, they each fasten their jaws in it and rip it apart with backward jerks of their head and shoulders. If younger ones are rash enough to dispute the food with their elders, they are driven away with a lunging rush. Nor are these sham attacks. Analyses of droppings show that the adults regularly eat the smaller ones. The dragon is also a cannibal.

A Komodo dragon's mouth is full of poisonous bacteria. One bite is enough to kill an animal with an infection, even if it does escape the Komodo's clutches.

Scientific name	*Varanus komodoensis*
Distribution	Islands of Komodo, Flores, Rinca and Padar
Habitat	Grassland
Size	3 metres including tail
Status	Vulnerable

SIBERIAN TIGER

from *Life of Pi*
by Yann Martel

His body, bright brownish orange streaked with black vertical stripes, was incomparably beautiful, matched with a tailor's eye for harmony by his pure white chest and underside and the black rings of his long tail. His head was large and round, displaying formidable sideburns, a stylish goatee and some of the finest whiskers in the cat world, thick, long and white. Atop the head were small expressive ears shaped like perfect arches. His carrot orange face had a broad bridge and a pink nose, and it was made up with brazen flair. Wavy dabs of black circled the face in a pattern that was striking yet subtle, for it brought less attention to itself than it did to the one part of the face left untouched by it, the bridge, whose rufous lustre shone nearly with a radiance. The patches of white above the eyes, on the cheeks and around the mouth came off as finishing touches, worthy of a Kathakali dancer. The result was a face that looked like the wings of a butterfly and bore an expression vaguely old and Chinese.

The Siberian tiger is the biggest cat. This huge hunter prowls the cold, snowy lands of eastern Asia. Thick fur keeps the tiger warm in the snow and ice, and the white in the coat helps the tiger to blend in with its snowy landscape.

Scientific name   *Panthera tigris altaica*
Distribution   Far Eastern Siberia
Habitat   Forest, coniferous woodlands
Size   2–3 metres including tail
Status   Critically Endangered

EURASIAN WATER SHREW

from *Some Account of the Water Shrew*
by John F M Dovaston

On a delicious evening, far in April, 1825, a little before sunset, strolling in my orchard, beside a pool, and looking into the clear water for insects I expected about that time to come out, I was surprised by seeing what I momentarily imagined to be a *Dyticus marginalia*, or some very large beetle, dart with rapid motion, and suddenly disappear. Laying myself down cautiously and motionless on the grass, I soon, to my delight and wonder, observed it was a mouse. I repeatedly marked it glide from the bank, under water, and bury itself in the mass of leaves at the bottom: I mean the leaves that had fallen off the trees in autumn, and which lay very thick over the mud. It very shortly returned, and entered the bank, occasionally putting its long sharp nose out of the water, and paddling close to the edge. This it repeated at very frequent intervals, from place to place, seldom going more than two yards from the side, and always returning in about half a minute. I presume it sought and obtained some insect or food among the rubbish and leaves, and retired to consume it. Sometimes it would run a little on the surface, and sometimes timidly and hastily come ashore, but with the

greatest caution, and instantly plunge in again. During the whole sweet spring of that fine year, I constantly visited my new acquaintance. When under water he looks grey, on account of the pearly cluster of minute air-bubbles that adhere to his fur, and bespangle him all over. His colour, however, is very dark brown, not quite so black as that of the mole, over the head and upper part of the body: the belly and throat are of the purest silvery white, with a dark spot under the tail: the ears are white at the edges, and very conspicuous; not from their prominence, being almost buried in the fur, but from contrast of colour...

He swims very rapidly; and, though he appears to dart, his very nimble wriggle is clearly discernible. He is never seen till near sunset, but I saw him, every evening I watched, with the most perfect facility. I believe this to be the animal said to be so long lost in England, the water-shrew.

This shrew has thick fur, which keeps it dry and warm when swimming underwater. It has hairs on its back feet and along its tail, which help the shrew to swim and steer.

Scientific name	*Neomys fodiens*
Distribution	Europe to northern Asia
Habitat	Damp woodlands, ponds, rivers
Size	Body: 6.5–9.5 centimetres
Status	Least Concern

PYGMY SHREW

from *In the Catskills*
by John Burroughs

The mice, too, how thick their tracks were, that of the white-footed mouse being most abundant; but occasionally there was a much finer track, with strides or leaps scarcely more than an inch apart. This is perhaps the little shrew-mouse of the woods, the body not more than an inch and a half long, the smallest mole or mouse kind known to me. Once, while encamping in the woods, one of these tiny shrews got into an empty pail standing in camp, and died before morning, either from the cold, or in despair of ever getting out of the pail.

Although shrews are widespread throughout the world, pygmy shrews are restricted to northern Europe. They have to eat every few hours or they starve to death.

Scientific name *Sorex minutus*
Distribution Northern Europe
Habitat Grassland, fields, hedges, farms, gardens, parks
Size Body: 4–6 centimetres
Status Least Concern

HAZEL DORMOUSE

from *Rewards and Fairies*
by Rudyard Kipling

'Oh, what about the sleeper you promised to show us?'
Dan cried.

''Ere he be – house an' all!' Hobden dived into the
prickly heart of the faggot and took out a dormouse's
wonderfully woven nest of grass and leaves. His blunt
fingers parted it as if it had been precious lace, and tilting
it toward the last of the light he showed the little, red,
furry chap curled up inside, his tail between his eyes that
were shut for their winter sleep.

'Let's take him home. Don't breathe on him,' said Una.
'It'll make him warm and he'll wake up and die straight
off. Won't he, Hobby?'

'Dat's a heap better by my reckonin' than wakin' up
and findin' himself in a cage for life. No! We'll lay him
into the bottom o' this hedge. Dat's jus' right! No more
trouble for him till come Spring. An' now we'll go home.'

*Dormice hibernate deeply in winter. They store food in their nest and
also in their bodies as fat to enable them to survive the cold months.*

Scientific name	*Muscardinus avellanarius*
Distribution	Europe
Habitat	Woodlands, shrubbery
Size	Body: 6–9 centimetres
Status	Near Threatened

WOOD MOUSE

'The Mouse in the Wainscot'
by Ian Serraillier

Hush, Suzanne!
don't lift your cup.
That breath you heard
is a mouse getting up.

As the mist that steams
from your milk as you sup,
so soft is the sound
of a mouse getting up.

There! did you hear
his feet pitter-patter,
lighter than tipping
of beads on a platter,

and then like a shower
on the window pane
the little feet scampering
back again?

O falling of feather!
O drift of a leaf!
The mouse in the wainscot
is dropping asleep.

These mice eat many different foods, including berries,
fruits, seeds, nuts and insects. In turn, they are a major
source of food for owls and other predators.

Scientific name *Apodemus sylvaticus*
Distribution Ireland, east to central Asia
Habitat Woods, hedgerows, gardens
Size Body: 8–13 centimetres
Status Least Concern

HARVEST MOUSE

from *Natural History of Selborne*
by Gilbert White

I have procured some of the mice mentioned in my former letters, a young one and a female with young, both of which I have preserved in brandy. From the colour, shape, size, and manner of nesting, I make no doubt but that the species is nondescript. They are much smaller, and more slender, than the *Mus domesticus medius* of Ray, and have more of the squirrel or dormouse colour; their belly is white, a straight line along their sides divides the shades of their back and belly. They never enter into houses; are carried into ricks and barns with the sheaves, abound in harvest; and build their nests amidst the straws of the corn above the ground, and sometimes in thistles. They breed as many as eight at a litter, in a little round nest composed of the blades of grass or wheat.

One of these nests I procured this autumn, most artificially platted, and composed of the blades of wheat, perfectly round, and about the size of a cricket ball, with the aperture so ingeniously closed, that there was no discovering to what part it belonged. It was so compact and well filled, that it would roll across the table without being discomposed, though it contained eight little mice that were naked and blind. As this nest was perfectly full, how could the dam come at her litter respectively, so as to administer a teat to each? Perhaps she opens different places for that purpose, adjusting them again when the business is over; but she could not possibly be contained herself in the ball with her young, which moreover would be daily increasing in bulk. This wonderful procreant cradle, an elegant instance of the efforts of instinct, was found in a wheat-field suspended in the head of a thistle.

This small mouse has an extraordinary tail, which it uses like a fifth limb. It can wrap its long tail around grass stems, using it for balance, climbing and grasping.

Scientific name	*Micromys minutus*
Distribution	Europe, eastern Russia, Korea, South China, northern India
Habitat	Dry grasslands, fields, hedgerows
Size	Body: 5.5–7.5 centimetres
Status	Near Threatened

AFRICAN ELEPHANT

from *The Devil's Dictionary*
by Ambrose Bierce

PROBOSCIS, *n.* The rudimentary organ of an elephant which serves him in place of the knife-and-fork that Evolution has as yet denied him. For purposes of humor it is popularly called a trunk.

These young elephants are part of a family group that is led by a female, or matriarch. If they are in danger, or scared, they rely on the matriarch to protect them.

Scientific name	*Loxodonta africana*
Distribution	Africa, south of the Sahara Desert
Habitat	Forest, savanna, grassland
Size	Body: 6–7.5 metres
Status	Vulnerable

FIELD VOLE

from *Creatures of the Night*
by Alfred W Rees

The night was mild and bright, and the vole was busy in the littered loam of the hedgerow, where, during the afternoon, a blackbird had scratched the leaves away and left some ripe haws exposed to view. Suddenly he heard a loud, mocking call, apparently coming from the direction of the moon: "Whoo-hoo! Whoo-hoo-o-o-o!" It was a strangely bewildering sound; so the vole squatted among the leaves and listened anxiously, every sense alert to catch the meaning of the weird, foreboding voice. "Whoo-hoo! Whoo-hoo-o-o-o!" again, from directly overhead, the cry rang out into the night. A low squeak of warning, uttered by the father vole as he dived into his burrow, caused the young mice foraging in the undergrowth to bolt helter-skelter towards home. Kweek, joining in the general panic, rushed across the field, and had almost disappeared underground when he felt the earth and the loose pebbles falling over him, and at the same time experienced a sharp thrill of pain. Fortunately, his speed saved him but only by an inch. The claws of the great brown owl, shutting like a vice as the bird "stooped" on her prey, laid hold of nothing but earth and grass, though one keen talon cut the vole's tail as with a knife, so that the little creature squealed lustily as he ran along the gallery to seek solace from his mother's companionship in the central chamber beyond. Yet even there he was not allowed to remain in peace. Maddened by the scent of a few drops of blood coming from his wound, the adult voles chased him from the burrow, and drove him out into the field. Luckily for him the brown owl had meanwhile flown away with another young vole in her claws. Kweek remained in safety under the haw-thorns till the grey dawn flushed the south-east sky; then, his injured tail having ceased to bleed, he ventured without fear among his kindred as they lay huddled asleep in the recesses of their underground abode.

The diet of field voles is mostly grass, so they live where they can find a plentiful supply. They will also eat fruits and nuts.

Scientific name *Microtus agrestis*
Distribution Europe
Habitat Rough grassland, woodland, fields, hedges
Size Body: 8–13 centimetres
Status Least Concern

EUROPEAN WATER VOLE

from *The Wind in the Willows*
by Kenneth Grahame

As he sat on the grass and looked across the river, a dark hole in the bank opposite, just above the water's edge, caught his eye, and dreamily he fell to considering what a nice snug dwelling-place it would make for an animal with few wants and fond of a bijou riverside residence, above flood level and remote from noise and dust. As he gazed, something bright and small seemed to twinkle down in the heart of it, vanished, then twinkled once more like a tiny star. But it could hardly be a star in such an unlikely situation; and it was too glittering and small for a glow-worm. Then, as he looked, it winked at him, and so declared itself to be an eye; and a small face began gradually to grow up round it, like a frame round a picture.

A brown little face, with whiskers.
A grave round face, with the same twinkle in its eye that had first attracted his notice.
Small neat ears and thick silky hair.
It was the Water Rat!

These voles eat plants growing by the water's edge and are excellent swimmers, both at the surface and under water.

Scientific name   *Arvicola amphibius*
                  (commonly called water rat)
Distribution   Europe, east to east Siberia and Mongolia
Habitat   Freshwater banks, grassland
Size   Body: 14–22.5 centimetres
Status   Least Concern

ARAB HORSE

from *The Horse: With a Treatise of Draught and a Copious Index*
by William Youatt

The Arabian Horse would not be acknowledged by every judge to possess a perfect form; His head, however, is inimitable. The broadness and squareness of the forehead, the shortness and fineness of the muzzle, the prominence and brilliancy of the eye, the smallness of the ears, and the beautiful course of the veins, will always characterise the head of the Arabian Horse…

Arabs are small horses but they are strong and instantly recognizable. They gallop with a wonderful, flowing movement and are famous for their stamina.

Scientific name	*Equus caballus*
Distribution	Worldwide
Habitat	Grassland
Size	1.4–1.55 metres to the shoulder
Status	Least Concern

Illustrator's note
"I've recently become a convert to using an airbrush, so trying effects such as this out-of-focus background have been a new challenge. Having always used a large brush in the past, this has given my work a new look."

30

In the Treetops

TOWNSEND'S BIG-EARED BAT

from 'Bat'
by D H Lawrence

Dark air-life looping
Yet missing the pure loop…
A twitch, a twitter, an elastic shudder in flight
And serrated wings against the sky,
Like a glove, a black glove thrown up at the light,
And falling back.

These bats emerge late in the evening and often travel large distances while foraging. Their prey includes small moths, flies, lacewings and dung beetles.

Scientific name	*Plecotus townsendii*
Distribution	Canada, Mexico, United States
Habitat	Rocky outcrops, caves, forests
Size	Body: 9–11 centimetres
Status	Vulnerable

33

PINE MARTEN

from *A History of Earth and Animated Nature*
by Oliver Goldsmith

Of all animals of the weasel kind, the martin is the most pleasing; all its motions show great grace, as well as agility; and there is scarcely an animal in our woods that will venture to oppose it. Quadrupeds five times as big are easily vanquished; the hare, the sheep, and even the wild cat itself, though much stronger, is not a match for the martin: and although carnivorous animals are not fond of engaging each other, yet the wild cat and the martin seldom meet without a combat… Gesner tells us of one of this kind that he kept tame, which was extremely playful and pretty; it went among the houses of the neighbour hood and always returned home when hungry: it was extremely fond of a dog that had been bred up with it, and used to play with it as cats are seen to play, lying on its back, and biting without anger or injury... It ate every thing that was given it, except salad or herbs; and it was remarkably fond of honey. It was remarked that it drank often, and often slept for two days together: and that, in like manner, it was often two or three days without sleeping. Before it went to sleep, it drew itself up into a round shape, hid its head, and covered itself with its tail.

Pine martens are excellent climbers and are often seen in trees, where they make their dens in holes and old squirrel nests. The bushy tail is used for balance in the branches.

Scientific name	*Martes martes*
Distribution	Europe to west and north Asia
Habitat	Woodlands, cliffs
Size	Body: 45–55 centimetres
Status	Least Concern

UAKARI MONKEY

from *The Life of Mammals*
by Sir David Attenborough

The red-faced uakari… has such a strange and dramatic appearance that catching sight of one suddenly and at close quarters in the forest of the Amazon can be almost alarming. Its colour is certainly one way by which members of the species recognize each other, but its particular shade also has a significance in an individual's social life. These monkeys live in groups of up to thirty. Each includes several adult males. The brilliance of their red faces and scalps varies from one to another. Research is now suggesting that the redder the male the more resistant he is to malaria. The brightest have never contracted the disease at all. Females, it has been discovered, prefer to mate with the males who have the brightest faces. By doing that, they ensure, no doubt unwittingly, that their offspring have a better chance of being malaria resistant than if they mated with the paler ones.

Uakaris are expert tree-climbers and they leap and swing from the branches. They forage in trees for flowers, fruits and small animals.

Scientific name *Cacajao calvus*
Distribution Western Brazil
Habitat Forest
Size Body: 51–57 centimetres
Status Near Threatened

AMERICAN BLACK BEAR

from 'The Bear'
by Robert Frost

The bear puts both arms around the tree above her
And draws it down as if it were a lover
And its chokecherries lips to kiss good-by,
Then lets it snap back upright in the sky.
Her next step rocks a boulder on the wall
(She's making her cross-country in the fall).
Her great weight creaks the barbed wire in its staples
As she flings over and off down through the maples,
Leaving on one wire tooth a lock of hair.
Such is the uncaged progress of the bear.
The world has room to make a bear feel free;
The universe seems cramped to you and me.

American black bears have short claws, which help them to grip tree trunks when climbing. Their diet is mainly plant-based, although they will also eat insects, carrion and small mammals.

Scientific name	*Ursus americanus*
Distribution	Canada, Mexico, United States
Habitat	Wooded areas, swamps, national parks
Size	Body: 1.5–1.8 metres
Status	Least Concern

Illustrator's note

"Working out to white gives a very dramatic feel to this design. Black fur is rarely completely black and it was hugely satisfying working on the form using the colours of the reflective light. The tree bark gave me the opportunity to work on interesting textures."

EASTERN GREY SQUIRREL

'Squirrel'
by Karen Fiser

If Durer had engraved this squirrel
It would be sober and poignant,
Or look that way. It would be darker
And thinner. This squirrel in the sun
Is flecked with gold, his skin
Is smooth and fat as my old hound's –
You could pinch up folds of it, rolling the fur
Between your thumb and forefinger.

This squirrel seems worldly, he makes sure
To keep one bright eye in my direction,
Like a man concerned about his wallet.
Rusty brown tail thinning to orange
At the edges, he's common, he's strong,
He's a worker with his hands,
Moving the nut nervously round and round
In his teeth, and then sideways,
As if to lick the thousandth envelope
Before knocking off for lunch. He's neither
Grave nor engraved. He's too busy
Being actual, sitting on a stumpy branch
Through a long afternoon in February.

Squirrels are great climbers and they scurry about in trees looking for food. They strip trees of their nuts and bury much of their hoard to eat later in the year.

Grey squirrels build large nests in the forks of tree branches. The outer frame of the nest is made from twigs, and the inside is then lined with leaves and grass. Old tree holes also provide ideal nesting conditions.

Scientific name	*Sciurus carolinensis*
Distribution	Southeast Canada, eastern USA; introduced to Britain and South Africa
Habitat	Hardwood forest
Size	Body: 23–30 centimetres
Status	Least Concern

YELLOWHAMMER

Anonymous

There he is (rat-tat-too!) yonder on the limb!
Cap of red upon his head drumming in the day.
(Five white eggs are hidden deep in a hollow dim!)
Heigho! heart of youth! Can't you hear him play?

Yellow-hammer, you and I in the long ago
Cronies were; (rat-tat-too down the morning tossed!)
Here's a hail across the years, – how they fleetly flow! –
Heigho! heart of youth! never wholly lost!

*The numbers of yellowhammers have declined in
recent years. The most likely reason for this is the loss
of habitat, which has reduced their food supply.*

Scientific name *Emberiza citrinella*
Distribution Europe, western Asia to Urals
Habitat Fields, farms, heaths, grasslands
Size 16 centimetres long
Status Least Concern

SISKIN

from *A History of British Birds*
by Francis Orpen Morris

Though inferior to the Goldfinch in beauty of plumage,
the Siskin is its equal in pleasing neatness – the one, as
it were, embodying the striking beauty of the orange,
and the other the more chastened and sober hue of the
lemon, in the general tone of its colour… If kept in
confinement the Siskin sometimes varies to white or
dusky, and Bechstein says that in very old males the
whole breast becomes black.

*In spring, male siskins sometimes perch at the
tops of trees, so their songs can carry further.*

Scientific name *Carduelis spinus*
Distribution Europe, Russia, eastern Asia
Habitat Conifer forests, gardens,
near rivers
Size 12 centimetres long
Status Least Concern

COMMON KESTREL

'The Meeting'
by A C Benson

The hawk slipt out of the pine, and rose in the sunlit air:
Steady and still he poised; his shadow slept on the grass:
And the bird's song sickened and sank: she cowered with furtive stare,
Dumb, till the quivering dimness should flicker and shift and pass.
Suddenly down he dropped: she heard the hiss of his wing,
Fled with a scream of terror: oh, would she had dared to rest!
For the hawk at eve was full, and there was no bird to sing,
And over the heather drifted the down from a bleeding breast.

Kestrels perch on telegraph poles or tall trees, looking for opportunities to feed on prey such as small mammals (especially voles), beetles, worms and small birds.

Scientific name	*Falco tinnunculus*
Distribution	Europe, Asia, Africa
Habitat	Woodlands, farms, heaths
Size	34–38 centimetres long
Status	Least Concern

Illustrator's note

"Birds are not one of my main subjects but I find satisfaction in painting the subtleties in the structure of feathers and the patterns they lie in. Different areas of feathers have various textures that give the bird it's lifelike look."

AYE-AYE

from *The Aye-Aye and I*
by Gerald Durrell

In the gloom it came along the branches towards me, its round, hypnotic eyes blazing, its spoon-like ears turning to and fro independently like radar dishes, its white whiskers twitching and moving like sensors; its black hands with their thin attenuated fingers, the third seeming prodigiously elongated, tapping delicately on the branches as it moved along, like those of a pianist playing a complicated piece by Chopin. It looked like a Walt Disney witch's black cat with a touch of ET thrown in for good measure. If ever a flying saucer came from Mars, you felt that this is what would emerge from it. It was Lewis Carroll's Jabberwocky come to life, whiffling through its tulgy wood.

The shaggy-haired aye-aye builds its nest in the forks of trees and emerges at night to eat insects and fruit. An aye-aye uses its long middle finger to probe into cracks in a tree and pick out tasty grubs to eat.

Scientific name	*Daubentonia madagascariensis*
Distribution	Formerly northeast Madagascar, now only in nature reserves
Habitat	Rainforest
Size	Body: 36–44 centimetres
Status	Endangered

RUFFED LEMUR

from *The Aye-Aye and I*
by Gerald Durrell

He drank until his little tummy was bulging, holding on to my hand with a vice-like grip and staring up into my face with wide, golden eyes. At that age lemurs heads, hands and feet are wildly out of proportion to their slender bodies and when they move on a flat surface they have the most comical Chaplinesque walk. When they climb into the branches, however, you realize that their outsize hands and feet are the most efficient grasping organs.

Like all lemurs, ruffed lemurs are excellent climbers. They scamper along branches, using their long tails to balance.

Scientific name	*Varecia variegata*
Distribution	Northeast and eastern Madagascar
Habitat	Rainforest
Size	Body: 60 centimetres
Status	Endangered

OWL MONKEY

'Sonnet to a Monkey'
by Marjorie Fleming aged 7

"O lively, O most charming pug!
Thy graceful air and heavenly mug!
The beauties of his mind do shine,
And every bit is shaped and fine.
Your teeth are whiter than the snow;
You're a great buck, you're a great beau;
Your eyes are of so nice a shape,
More like a Christian's than an ape;
Your cheek is like the rose's blume;
Your hair is like the raven's plume;
His nose's cast is of the Roman:
He is a very pretty woman.
I could not get a rhyme for Roman,
So was obliged to call him woman."

Owl monkeys are the only nocturnal monkeys.
They sleep in hollow trees during the day, and at
night they clamber through the branches, eating
a diet of fruits, leaves and insects.

Scientific name	*Aotus trivirgatus*
Distribution	Panama to Paraguay (patchy distribution)
Habitat	Forest
Size	Body: 24–37 centimetres
Status	Least Concern

Weaver birds get their name from the complex, elaborately woven nests that they make. The nests vary in shape, size, material and construction. Males use their nest-building skills to attract a mate.

BAYA WEAVER BIRDS

from *Homes without Hands. Being a Description of the Habitations of Animals* by John George Wood

Although the majority of nest-making birds may be called Weavers, there is one family to which the name is par excellence and with justice applied. These are the remarkable birds which are grouped together under the name of Ploceidae, all being inhabitants of the hot portions of the old world, such as Asia and Africa. The last-mentioned continent is peculiarly rich in Weaver Birds... For the most part, the Weaver Birds suspend their nests to the ends of twigs, small branches, drooping parasites, palm-leaves, or reeds, and many species always hang their nests over water, and at no very great height above its surface. The object of this curious locality is evidently that the eggs and young should be saved from the innumerable monkeys that swarm in the forests, and whose filching paws would rob many a poor bird of its young brood. As, however, the branches are very slender, the weight of the monkey, however small the animal may be, is more than sufficient to immerse the would-be thief in the water and so to put a stop to his marauding propensities. It is well known that the monkey race are very fond of a little bird, mouse, or egg, and that they have such a predilection for blood, that they will snatch the feathers out of parrots' tails, in order to suck the raw and bleeding quills. Snakes, too, also inveterate nest-robbers, some of them living almost exclusively on young birds and eggs, are effectually debarred from entering the nests, so that the parent birds need not trouble themselves about either foe. Although they may repose in perfect safety, undismayed by the approach of either snake or monkey, they never can see one of their enemies without scolding at it, screaming hoarsely, shooting close to its body, and, if possible, indulging in a passing peck.

Scientific name	*Ploceus philippinus*
Distribution	India, Sri Lanka to southwest China, parts of Southeast Asia, Sumatra, Java
Habitat	Cultivated land, grassland, secondary scrub
Size	15 centimetres long
Status	Least Concern

Snow
and Ice

HARBOUR SEAL

from *Moby-Dick*
by Herman Melville

Those rocky islands the ship had passed were the resort of great numbers of seals, and some young seals that had lost their dams, or some dams that had lost their cubs, must have risen nigh the ship and kept company with her, crying and sobbing with their human sort of wail. But this only the more affected some of them, because most mariners cherish a very superstitious feeling about seals, arising not only from their peculiar tones when in distress, but also from the human look of their round heads and semi-intelligent faces, seen peeringly uprising from the water alongside. In the sea, under certain circumstances, seals have more than once been mistaken for men.

The harbour, or common, seal feeds primarily on fish.
It will also prey upon crustaceans and molluscs such as
squid. Dives to catch prey usually last 3–4 minutes.

Scientific name *Phoca vitulina*
Distribution North Atlantic and North Pacific Oceans
Habitat Temperate and subarctic coastal waters
Size 1.4–1.8 metres long
Status Least Concern

SHETLAND PONY

from *Chambers Encyclopedia 1863*

The Shetland Pony, which, compared with the dray-horse, is like a pocket edition of a book beside a great folio, is most prized when most diminutive, and sometimes does not much exceed a large dog in stature. A strong man has been seen to lift one with his arm, and again to ride on its back, whilst at the same time he walked with his feet on each side on the ground. The Shetland Pony is, however, a very hardy animal, and remarkably strong.

Shetland ponies have long, thick fur and manes to protect them from the cold. They are incredibly hardy and, considering their small size, they are probably the strongest of all horses and ponies.

Scientific name   *Equus caballus*
Distribution   Shetland Islands
Habitat   Grassland
Size   1.07 metres to the shoulder
Status   Least Concern

Illustrator's note
"This is my favourite scene in the book. I particularly enjoy painting snow and the colours in this picture, with the strong shadows, were very pleasing to create."

ROCKHOPPER PENGUIN

from *A Voyage Towards the South Pole*
by James Weddell

In pride, these birds are perhaps not surpassed even by the peacock, to which in beauty of plumage they are indeed very little inferior – as may be seen in our principal museums. During the time of moulting, they seem to repel each other with disgust, on account of the ragged state of their coats; but as they arrive at the maximum of splendour they re-assemble, and no one who has not completed his plumage is allowed to enter the community. They are frequently looking down their front and sides in order to contemplate the perfection of their exterior brilliancy, and to remove any speck which might sully it, is truly amusing to an observer.

Rockhoppers are one of the smallest species of crested penguins. They are so-called due to their habit of jumping from boulder to boulder when moving around their colonies.

Scientific name   *Eudyptes chrysocome*
Distribution   Subantarctic waters of western Pacific and Indian Oceans, southern coasts of South America
Habitat   Grassy, rocky shores
Size   55 centimetres tall
Status   Vulnerable

ADELIE PENGUIN

from *The South Pole*
by Roald Amundsen

Penguins had not shown themselves particularly often, only a few here and there; but we appreciated them all the more. The few we saw were almost all Adelie penguins. While we were at work making the ship fast, a flock of them suddenly shot up out of the water and on to the ice. They looked about them in surprise for a moment: men and ships do not come their way every day. But it seemed as if their astonishment soon gave way to a desire to see what was happening. They positively sat and studied all our movements. Only now and then they grunted a little and took a turn over the ice. What specially interested them was evidently our work at digging holes in the snow for the grapnels. They flocked about the men who were engaged in this, laid their heads on one side, and looked as if they found it immensely interesting. They did not appear to be the least afraid of us, and for the most part we left them in peace.

Adult Adelies are small, but they are able to survive in one of the harshest places on Earth. Around five million adult Adelies live in the Antarctic, often in huge groups that number tens of thousands.

Scientific name   *Pygoscelis adeliae*
Distribution   Antarctica
Habitat   Coastal areas
Size   70 centimetres tall
Status   Least Concern

EMPEROR PENGUIN

from *The Worst Journey in the World*
by Apsley Cherry-Garrard

They are extraordinarily like children, these little people of the Antarctic world, either like children, or like old men, full of their own importance and late for dinner, in their black tail-coats and white shirt-fronts – and rather portly withal.

The Emperor is the biggest species of penguin. Its body is well adapted to the incredibly cold conditions, and its dense feathers and layer of body fat help to counteract heat loss.

Scientific name	*Aptenodytes forsteri*
Distribution	Antarctic coasts
Habitat	Ocean and pack ice
Size	1.2 metres tall
Status	Least Concern

EURASIAN LYNX

from *A History of the Earth and Animated Nature*
by Oliver Goldsmith

This animal has been called by some *Lupus ceniarius*, or a creature compounded between a wolf and a stag; but for what reason, is hard to guess; it no way resembles either, in shape or in disposition. In its nature, it exactly resembles the cat, except that being bigger, and nearly two feet long, it is bolder and fiercer. Like the cat, it climbs trees, and seeks its prey by surprise; like the cat, it is delicate and cleanly, covering its urine with its paws; and it resembles the wolf in nothing except its cry, which often deceives the hunters, and induces them to think they hear a wolf and not a lynx. This animal also is rather more delicate than the cat; and after having once feasted upon its prey, will never return to it again, but hunts the woods for another. From hence may have arisen the common report of the lynx having, of all other quadrupeds, the shortest memory.

The lynx is characterized by its tufted ears and its short black-tipped tail. Its thick fur coat can vary in colour from pale grey to brown. The lynx's paws are large and wide to prevent it sinking into the soft snow, or sliding on the ice.

Scientific name	*Lynx lynx*
Distribution	Europe: Scandinavia, east through Asia to Siberia
Habitat	Coniferous forest, scrub
Size	1–1.3 metres including tail
Status	Near Threatened

ARCTIC GROUND SQUIRREL

from *Adventure Guide Alaska Highway*
by Ed and Lynn Readicker-Henderson

Along this section of the road, watch closely for Arctic ground squirrels. They live in small tunnels and take great delight in running in front of cars. Looking rather like fat prairie dogs, they are the favourite food of many Northern predators, and there are seemingly billions of the bite-sized critters, so everybody can chow down. If you really wonder, we can tell you from experience: boiled Arctic ground squirrel tastes a lot like – no, not chicken: dark turkey meat.

In Denali Park, the Arctic ground squirrel is the main source of meat protein for the Toklat grizzlies, despite the fact that one squirrel provides only around 2000 calories. If a grizzly bear can catch a six-pack or so of squirrels, it's had a pretty good day.

The Arctic ground squirrel hibernates for up to seven months of the year. When it emerges from its burrow, it feeds on a variety of plants, seeds and berries.

Scientific name	*Spermophilus parryii*
Distribution	Northern Canada, Alaska, Siberia
Habitat	Dry Arctic tundra, open meadows
Size	39 centimetres tall
Status	Least Concern

MOUNTAIN HARE

from *Wikipedia, The Free Encyclopedia*

The Mountain Hare is the provincial animal of Medelpad in Sweden.

In northern parts of Finland and Sweden, the Mountain Hare and the European Hare compete for habitat. The European Hare, being larger, is usually able to drive away the Mountain Hare but is less adapted for living in snowy regions: its feet are smaller and its winter fur is a mixture of white and brown. While this winter fur is actually a very good camouflage in the coastal regions of Finland where the snow covers the shrubs but for a short time, the Mountain Hare is better adapted for the snowier conditions of the inland areas.

The mountain hare's winter coat is completely white, except for the ear tips, which remain black. The summer coat is brown with a blue tinge. The tail stays white throughout the year.

Scientific name	*Lepus timidus*
Distribution	Europe, North Africa, North Asia
Habitat	Forests, moorlands
Size	Body: 45–66 centimetres
Status	Least Concern

SNOW LEOPARD

from *The Snow Leopard*
by Peter Matthiessen

The typical snow leopard has pale frosty eyes and a coat of pale misty grey, with black rosettes that are clouded by the depth of the rich fur. An adult rarely weighs more than a hundred pounds or exceeds six feet in length, including the remarkable long tail, thick to the tip, used presumably for balance and for warmth, but it kills creatures three times its own size without much difficulty. It has enormous paws and a short-faced heraldic head, like a leopard of myth; it is bold and agile in the hunt and capable of terrific leaps; and although its usual prey is the blue sheep, it occasionally takes livestock, including young yak of several hundred pounds. This means that man would be fair game as well, although no attack on a human being has ever been reported.

The snow leopard is the most mysterious of the great cats; of its social system, there is nothing known. Almost always it is seen alone; it may meet over a kill, as tigers do, or it may be unsociable and solitary, like a true leopard.

The snow leopard lives in the high mountains of Central Asia. It has short, stocky limbs for climbing and its tail helps it to balance on rocky surfaces. When it sleeps, the snow leopard wraps its thick tail around its body to prevent heat escaping.

Scientific name	*Uncia uncia*
Distribution	Pakistan, Afghanistan, Himalayas, east to China
Habitat	Mountain slopes, forest
Size	2–2.5 metres including tail
Status	Endangered

Illustrator's note

"I really like painting fur and feathers as it involves using challenging techniques. I enjoy creating the fine detail and building up the textures on the animal's coat."

60

WEDDELL SEAL

from *The White Seal*
by Rudyard Kipling

He was always learning. Matkah taught him to follow the cod and the halibut along the under sea banks, and wrench the rockling out of his hole among the weeds; how to skirt the wrecks lying a hundred fathoms below water, and dart like a rifle-bullet in at one porthole and out at another as the fishes ran; how to dance on top of the waves when the lightning was racing all over the sky, and wave his flipper politely to the stumpy-tailed albatross and the Man-of-war hawk as they went down the wind; how to jump three or four feet clear of the water like a dolphin, flippers close to the side and tail curved; to leave the flying fish alone because they are all bony; to take the shoulder piece out of a piece of cod at full speed ten fathoms deep; and never to stop and look at a boat or ship, but particularly a row boat. At the end of six months what Kotick did not know about deep-sea fishing was not worth the knowing, and all that time he never set flipper on dry ground.

Weddel seals can dive to depths of 500 metres for up to one hour to find prey. They make breathing holes by bashing their noses, teeth and flippers against the thin ice.

Scientific name *Leptonychotes weddelli*
Distribution Antarctic
Habitat Edge of pack ice
Size 2.5–3.5 metres long
Status Least Concern

Family
Life

TIGER

from The *Expression of the Emotions in Man and Animals*
by Charles Darwin

Cats use their voices much as a means of expression, and they utter, under various emotions and desires, at least six or seven different sounds. The purr of satisfaction, which is made during both inspiration and expiration, is one of the most curious. The puma, cheetah, and ocelot likewise purr; but the tiger, when pleased, emits a peculiar short snuffle, accompanied by the closure of the eyelids.

A young tiger is completely dependent on its mother for food for the first year of its life. By the time the cub is two years old it will have enough strength and experience to catch prey for itself.

Scientific name	*Panthera tigris*
Distribution	Siberia to Java and Bali
Habitat	Forest
Size	1.8–3 metres including tail
Status	Endangered

EASTERN GREY KANGAROO

from 'Kangaroo'
by D H Lawrence

Delicate mother Kangaroo
Sitting up there rabbit-wise, but huge, plumb-weighted,
And lifting her beautiful slender face, oh! so much more
    gently and finely lined than a rabbit's, or than a hare's,
Lifting her face to nibble at a round white peppermint drop
    which she loves, sensitive mother Kangaroo.

Her sensitive, long, pure-bred face.
Her full antipodal eyes, so dark,
So big and quiet and remote, having watched so many
    empty dawns in silent Australia.

Her little loose hands, and drooping Victorian shoulders.
And then her great weight below the waist, her vast pale belly,
With a thin young yellow little paw hanging out, and
    straggle of a long thin ear, like ribbon,
Like a funny trimming to the middle of her belly, thin
    little dangle of an immature paw, and one thin ear.

Her belly, her big haunches
And, in addition, the great muscular python-stretch of her tail.

There, she shan't have any more peppermint drops.
So she wistfully, sensitively sniffs the air, and then turns,
    goes off in sad slow leaps
On the long flat skis of her legs,
Steered and propelled by that steel-strong snake of a tail.

A baby kangaroo, called a joey, lives in its mother's pocket-shaped pouch for the first six months of its life. It feeds on her milk until it is strong enough to leave the pouch and explore.

Scientific name	*Macropus giganteus*
Distribution	Australia
Habitat	Open grassland, bushes
Size	1.6–2 metres tall
Status	Least Concern

EMPEROR PENGUIN

'Emperor Penguins'
by Barry Louis Polisar

Huddled close together
Against the snow and sleet,
Penguins at the pole
Pool their body heat.

They gather in a circle,
Steadfast, disciplined,
Turning toward the center,
Fighting off the wind.

Sharing warmth and comfort
On cold and icy floes,
Balancing their future
Gently on their toes.

Emperor penguin chicks sit on the males' feet and are sheltered by their belly feathers. As they grow older, chicks grow fluffy feathers and they huddle together for extra warmth in the icy wind.

Scientific name	*Aptenodytes forsteri*
Distribution	Antarctic coasts
Habitat	Ocean and pack ice
Size	1.2 metres tall
Status	Least Concern

SILVERED LANGUR MONKEY

from *The Book of Beasts: Being a Translation from a Latin Bestiary of the Twelfth Century* by T H White

They are called monkeys (Simia) in the Latin language because people notice a great similitude to human reason in them. Wise in the lore of the elements, these creatures grow merry at the time of the new moon. At half and full moon, they are depressed. Such is the nature of a monkey that when she gives birth to twins, she esteems one of them highly but scorns the other. Hence, if it ever happens that she gets chased by a sportsman she clasps the one she likes in her arms in front of her, and carries the one she detests with its arms around her neck, pickaback. But for this very reason, when she is exhausted by running on her hind legs, she has to throw away the one she loves and carries the one she hates, willy-nilly… Admitting that the whole of a monkey is disgraceful, yet their bottoms really are excessively disgraceful and horrible.

Silvered langurs have silver-grey fur, but their babies are born bright orange. After three months, this striking colour fades as grey fur grows. The youngsters may look so different to remind older langurs to treat them more gently.

Scientific name	*Trachypithecus cristatus* (also known as silvered leaf monkey)
Distribution	Southeast Asia and Indonesia
Habitat	Forests and swamps
Size	Body: 45–55 centimetres
Status	Not evaluated

PROBOSCIS MONKEY

from *The Lonely Planet Guide to Malaysia, Singapore and Brunei*
by Simon Richmond

The fantastic proboscis monkey is a type of langur and is probably Malaysia's second-most-famous animal, after the orang-utan. The male proboscis monkey is an improbable-looking creature with a pendulous nose and bulbous belly; females and youngsters are more daintily built with quaint, upturned noses.

Although baby proboscis monkeys are born with normal-sized noses, they soon start to grow, and by the time they are adult males, proboscis monkeys have long, droopy snouts. The male has a bigger nose than the female – it can be up to 8 centimetres in length.

Scientific name	*Nasalis larvatus*
Distribution	Borneo
Habitat	Mangroves, riverbanks
Size	Body: 53–76 centimetres
Status	Endangered

FALLOW DEER FAWN

from *Concerning Animals and
Other Matters*
by E H Aitken

The eyes of a fawn are lustrous and
beautiful, but they would be as meaningless
as polished stones without the eloquent ears
that stand behind them and tell her
thoughts. Curiosity, suspicion, alarm, anger,
submission, friendliness, every emotion that
flits across her quick, sensitive mind speaks
through them. They are in touch with her
soul, and half the music of her life is played
on them.

*The fawn lies in thick vegetation while its mother feeds.
It stays still and silent and is camouflaged from predators
by its spotted coat, which blends in with patches of
sunlight on the ground. The doe visits her baby to feed it
on her milk, and then she returns to the herd.*

Scientific name *Dama dama*
Distribution Europe
Habitat Woodlands
Size 85–100 centimetres
to the shoulder
Status Least Concern

71

AFRICAN ELEPHANT

from *On the Origin of Species*
by Charles Darwin

The elephant is reckoned to be the slowest breeder of all known animals, and I have taken some pains to estimate its probable minimum rate of natural increase: it will be under the mark to assume that it breeds when thirty years old, and goes on breeding till ninety years old, bringing forth three pair of young in this interval; if this be so, at the end of the fifth century there would be alive fifteen million elephants, descended from the first pair.

A mother elephant constantly touches her baby with her trunk. The calf stays close to its mother for the first year or two. It is protected by all members of the herd, which are usually blood relatives.

Scientific name	*Loxodonta africana*
Distribution	Africa, south of the Sahara Desert
Habitat	Forest, savanna, grassland
Size	Body: 6–7.5 metres
Status	Vulnerable

CHINSTRAP PENGUIN

from *The Living Planet*
by Sir David Attenborough

On Zavodovski, a small volcanic island in the South Sandwich group only 6 kilometres across, 14 million pairs of chinstrap penguins nest. They are small creatures, standing no higher than a man's knees. At the beginning of the Antarctic summer they come in to land, the huge swell hurling them on to the rocks with such violence that they seem certain to be smashed. But they have the resilience of rubber balls and as the surf drains back from the rocks it leaves them unharmed and undismayed and they waddle perkily inland. There on the bare volcanic ash they excavate simple scoops, squabbling ferociously and with ear-splitting shrieks over the pebbles with which they line them. In these meagre scrapes they lay two eggs. The male incubates them while the female goes down to feed. If, as sometimes happens, the pair have chosen to nest in a gully where the ash is underlain by ice, then the heat of his body will melt the ice which drains away leaving him with his eggs sitting, in a rather bewildered way, in a deep hole.

Parent birds feed their chicks by regurgitating food from their crops (a stomach-like pouch in their throat). Food passes from the parents' crop to its bill, and then into a chick's open mouth. Young penguins, such as these chinstrap chicks, peck at an adult's mouth to encourage them to regurgitate their food.

Scientific name	*Pygoscelis antarcticus*
Distribution	Antarctica
Habitat	Coastal areas
Size	71–76 centimetres tall
Status	Least Concern

EURASIAN OTTER

from *The Water Babies*
by Charles Kingsley

Suddenly, Tom heard the strangest noise up the stream; cooing, and grunting, and whining, and squeaking, as if you had put into a bag two stock-doves, nine mice, three guinea-pigs, and a blind puppy, and left them there to settle themselves and make music.

He looked up the water, and there he saw a sight as strange as the noise; a great ball rolling over and over down the stream, seeming one moment of soft brown fur, and the next of shining glass: and yet it was not a ball; for sometimes it broke up and streamed away in pieces, and then it joined again; and all the while the noise came out of it louder and louder.

Tom asked the dragon-fly what it could be: but, of course, with his short sight, he could not even see it, though it was not ten yards away. So he took the neatest little header into the water, and started off to see for himself; and, when he came near, the ball turned out to be four or five beautiful creatures, many times larger than Tom, who were swimming about, and rolling, and diving, and twisting, and wrestling, and cuddling, and kissing, and biting, and scratching, in the most charming fashion that ever was seen. And if you don't believe me, you may go to the Zoological Gardens (for I am afraid that you won't see it nearer, unless, perhaps, you get up at five in the morning, and go down to Cordery's Moor, and watch by the great withy pollard which hangs over the backwater, where the otters breed sometimes), and then say, if otters at play in the water are not the merriest, lithest, gracefullest creatures you ever saw.

Otter babies love to play. They roll, tumble and jump in the riverbank mud. Sometimes they have pretend fights, and this is practice for when they have to hunt their own food. By the time they are four months old they can catch fish, baby frogs and waterbird chicks.

Scientific name	*Lutra lutra*
Distribution	Europe, North Africa, Asia
Habitat	Rivers, lakes, sheltered coasts
Size	Body: 55–80 centimetres
Status	Near Threatened

ORANG-UTAN

from *The Expression of the Emotions in Man and Animals*
by Charles Darwin

Many years ago, in the Zoological Gardens, I placed a looking-glass on the floor before two young orangs, who, as far as it was known, had never before seen one. At first they gazed at their own images with the most steady surprise, and often changed their point of view. They then approached close and protruded their lips towards the image, as if to kiss it, in exactly the same manner as they had previously done towards each other, when first placed, a few days before, in the same room. They next made all sorts of grimaces, and put themselves in various attitudes before the mirror; they pressed and rubbed the surface; they placed their hands at different distances behind it; looked behind it; and finally seemed almost frightened, started a little, became cross, and refused to look any longer.

Young orang-utans remain with their mothers until they are about eight years old – longer than all other primates, except humans. They feed on their mother's milk for three years or more. The mother protects her baby from predators, such as large eagles.

Scientific name	*Pongo pygmaeus* and *Pongo abelii*
Distribution	Borneo, Sumatra
Habitat	Rainforest
Size	0.8–1.8 metres tall
Status	Endangered

GREY WOLF

from *Shasta of the Wolves*
by Olaf Baker

It was the old she-wolf Nitka that came running lightly along the dusk. Though she had a great and powerful body, with a weight heavy enough to bear down a grown man, her feet made no sound as they came padding through the trees. She had been a long way, travelling for a kill, because at home the wolf-babies were very hungry and gave her no peace. They were not well-behaved babies at all. Whatever mischief there was in the world seemed to be packed tight into their little furry bodies. They played and fought and worried each other till they grew hungry again, and then they fell upon their mother like the little ravening monsters that they were. But Nitka bore it all patiently, as a kind old mother should, and only gave them a smack occasionally, when their behaviour was beyond everything for naughtiness.

Now, as she came running through the trees she drank in the air thirstily through her long nose. For it was her nose that brought her news of the forest, telling her what creatures were abroad, and whether there was a chance of a kill. This evening the air was full of smells, and heavy with the heat of the long summer day; but many of them were wood smells, tree smells, green smells; not the scent of the warm fur and the warm flesh and the good blood that ran in the warm bodies and made them spill the secret of themselves along the air. And it was this warm, red, running smell for which Nitka was so thirsty, and of which there was so little spilt upon the creeping dusk. Yet now and then a delicate whiff of it would come, and Nitka would sniff harder, swinging her head into the wind. And sometimes it grew stronger and sometimes weaker, and sometimes would cease altogether, swallowed up in the scent of the things that were green. And then, all of a sudden, the smell came thick and strong, flowing like a stream along the drift of the air.

In the wild, your scent is yourself. What you smell like, that you are. And so, accordingly as the wind blows, you spill yourself, even against your will, either backwards or forwards, on the currents of the air.

For the first few weeks of their lives, grey wolf cubs remain inside the den, where their mother feeds them with milk. They then begin to explore outside and start to eat meat, which is brought to them by other members of the pack.

Scientific name	*Canis lupus*
Distribution	North America, Greenland, eastern Europe, Asia
Habitat	Tundra, steppe, open woodland, forest
Size	Body: 1–1.4 metres
Status	Least Concern

SLOTH BEAR

from *The Great and Small Game of India, Burma and Tibet*
by Richard Lydekker

With the exception of the snout, which is a dirty grey, of a narrow white horseshoe-shaped gorget on the chest, and of the white claws, the sloth bear is an entirely black animal; the long and shaggy hair, which attains a greater degree of elongation over the shoulders than elsewhere gives such a generally untidy appearance that not even its best friend could say it was a comely or graceful creature. In point of fact, it is downright ugly, although, no doubt, an admirable member of ursine society…

As an illustration of the power of these animals, it may be mentioned that during the winter of 1897–98 an encounter took place between a polar bear and an Indian sloth-bear at Sanger's Circus, in which the latter came off an easy victor. It seems at first sight remarkable that such a powerful animal as a polar bear should have been so easily vanquished, but it was the cruelly long claws of the Indian that doubtless did the business, while the length and shagginess of his coat would protect him from the teeth and shorter talons of his northern antagonist.

Sloth bear cubs can be born at any time of year, and there are normally one or two cubs in a litter. The cubs emerge from their den when they are three months old, and the mother carries them on her back until they are nine months old.

Scientific name *Melursus ursinus*
Distribution Bangladesh, India, Nepal, Sri Lanka
Habitat Forest, desert, open habitats
Size Body: 1.4–1.8 metres
Status Vulnerable

SPECTACLED BEAR

from *Rescuing the Spectacled Bear*
by Stephen Fry

The Spectacled Bear, *Tremarctos ornatus* of the family Ursidae, is the only bear native to South America. They are officially classed as carnivores, but this is a confusing taxonomical anomaly that says more about zoologists than bears, since they are almost exclusively eaters of fruit, cereals, succulents, cacti and bromeliads (spiny fruit plants like the pineapple). Because they will also munch on an ant from time to time, they are described as meat-eaters. Devourers of flesh who also nibble the odd blade of grass do not get classified as herbivores, but that is something for biologists to explain.

The Spectacled Bear inhabits the coastal and inland deserts, dry forest, rain forest, cloud forest, steppe, and paramo of Ecuador, Peru, Colombia, Bolivia, and possibly Brazil, usually at altitudes between 1900 m and 2350 m. They have been seen as far south as the Bolivian/Argentine border and as far north as the Colombian/Panamanian border, though few believe there are resident populations in either Panama or Argentina. They are at their most populous on the eastern slopes of the Andes that run down from Ecuador through Peru to northern Bolivia.

Their name derives from the yellowish marking around the eyes that become more accentuated with maturity in both sexes. To sight them is a rarity for several reasons: they are mostly nocturnal, sleeping by day and foraging by night. They have a magnificent sense of smell and are excessively shy, which means they will have detected the presence of Man a long time before Man will have detected the presence of Bear. We heard, during our time in Peru, several stories of experienced natural history film-makers who had spent six months following tracks and droppings, only to retire beaten without a single frame of bear-rich footage.

Mother spectacled bears build dens for their cubs, often in tree roots or under rocks. They make unusual noises to communicate with their cubs including screeching and soft purring sounds.

Scientific name	*Tremarctos ornatus*
Distribution	South America: Venezuela, Colombia, Ecuador, Peru, Western Bolivia
Habitat	Forest, savanna, mountainous areas up to 3000 metres
Size	Body: 1.5–1.8 metres
Status	Vulnerable

GIANT PANDA

from *Panda, Inc.*
by Lynne Warren

He's got chubby cheeks. He naps a lot. He eats with his hands. He lives with his mother. Not exactly the kind of character you'd expect to find at the center of high finance, international diplomacy, fan frenzy, government scrutiny, and scientific fascination. But Tai Shan is a giant panda cub, and that makes him, well, not your average bear…

What makes pandas so special? Could be sheer cuteness. Giant pandas possess the charisma that politicians and movie stars dream of—and people crave a glimpse. The National Zoo's Internet panda cams, which follow the daily activities of Tai Shan and his mom, draw an average of two million online visits a month. In the first three months that Tai Shan was on public display, visits to the zoo jumped by as much as 50 percent over prior years. Adoring fans pack the railing at the Giant Panda Habitat shoulder to shoulder. Fingers point, voices coo, faces crease in blissful grins. So many cameras click at once that you'd think you were on the red carpet on Oscar night.

Scarcity also boosts the bears' cachet. Giant pandas are excruciatingly rare. Even other famously endangered mammals—tigers, gorillas, black rhinos, Asian elephants—outnumber them, both in the wild and in captivity. China's most recent national giant panda survey reported that 1590 of the black-and-white bears survive in the rugged hills of Sichuan, Shaanxi, and Gansu Provinces. Such a precise figure is questionable, especially for a hard-to-spot species that occupies isolated and often virtually impassable mountain forests. Wildlife biologists put the free-ranging population somewhere between 1000 and 2000 individuals. In captivity, there were only 188 pandas worldwide at the end of 2005: the 11 U.S. residents, a handful of others in Mexico, Japan, Thailand, Germany, and Austria, and all the rest in zoos and research centers in their native China.

The female panda usually gives birth to just one cub, but sometimes she has two. The newborn cub is entirely helpless, but by six weeks old it can leave its den and follow its mother. At six months old, the cub is eating bamboo, its favourite food. The young panda stays with its mother for over a year.

Scientific name	*Ailuropoda melanoleuca*
Distribution	Mountains of central China
Habitat	Bamboo forest
Size	Body: 1.2–1.5 metres
Status	Endangered

LION

from *The Heart of the Hunter*
by Laurens van der Post

That night we heard our last lion. He was just the right distance from us to make the sound of his roar perfect. I have always been grateful that I was born into a world and shall die in one where the lion, however diminished in number, is still roaring. Heard in his and my native setting, it is for me the most beautiful sound in the world. It is to silence what the shooting star is to the dark of the night. All that black night long the roar of the lion came and went around our camp, and ceased finally only at dawn. The spoor of the lion by first sunlight was one of the biggest any of us had ever seen, and completely circled our fire.

Lions are the only big cats that live together. They form close-knit social groups, consisting of mostly mothers with their young, and one or two males. These groups are called prides.

Scientific name *Panthera leo*
Distribution Africa, south of the Sahara Desert, northwest India, south Asia
Habitat Open savanna
Size 2.4–3 metres including tail
Status Vulnerable

CHIMPANZEE

from *The Bafut Beagles*
by Gerald Durrell

Charlie had been the pet of a planter before he came to us so he was fairly domesticated. He had a small, wrinkled, sorrowful face and melting brown eyes; he looked as though the world had treated him harshly but that he was too much of a saint to complain. This wounded, dejected air was a lot of moonshine, for in reality Charlie, far from being an ill-treated, misunderstood ape was a disgraceful little street urchin, full of low cunning and deceit. Every day we used to let him out of his cage for exercise, and he would roam about the camp looking radiantly innocent until he thought he had lulled you into believing in his integrity. Then he would wander nonchalantly towards the food table, give a quick glance round to see if he was observed, grab the largest bunch of bananas within reach and dash madly away towards the nearest tree. If you gave chase, he would drop the fruit and skid to a standstill. Then he would sit in the dust while you scolded him, gazing up at you sorrowfully, the picture of injured innocence, the expression on his face showing quite plainly that he was being wrongly accused of a monstrous crime about that he was far too noble to point it out to you if you were too obtuse to realize it.

Young primates spend a lot of time with adults, watching and learning. Youngsters, such as this chimp, don't know how to use tools such as leaves and sticks naturally – they only find out by watching adults and copying them.

Scientific name	*Pan troglodytes*
Distribution	Africa: Guinea to Democratic Republic of Congo (DRC), Uganda and Tanzania
Habitat	Rainforest, savanna with woodland
Size	Body: 68–94 centimetres
Status	Endangered

Illustrator's note
"I loved capturing the expression on this chimp's face and the light in its eyes making it appear to be looking at you."

RED FOX

from *Lakeland Gray*
by Richard Clapham

The place which in her wisdom she had chosen for them was a roomy space behind two large boulders, the only access being through a narrow crevice between the rocks. She could squeeze her way in to them, but it would have taken a small and narrow-chested terrier to have passed the entrance. Almost on a level with the latter, earth and small stones formed a broad shelf on which the cubs could bask and play, while no human intruder could approach without being seen by their watchful mother. After licking the cub with her tongue, she slipped away and headed down-hill. During that moonlight night she carried all four cubs to their new abode, and when at last her task was finished, the dawn was breaking in the east.

A day or two before they left their birth-place she had brought their first flesh food, a baby rabbit. The cubs fell upon it like little furies, the fur and meat combined arousing all their hunting instinct. Even at that tender age they growled and hissed at each other as they fed, for their table manners were not nice. They had grown, and their eyes were assuming the amber hue of the eyes of an adult fox. Their coats, too, were beginning to change from mouse colour to brown, and their little flesh-coloured noses had turned black.

The female fox, or vixen, makes a den in a sheltered place in which to have her cubs. Here, a litter of 4–8 cubs is born in March. The cubs are fully independent after six months.

Scientific name	*Vulpes vulpes*
Distribution	Arctic, North America, Europe, Asia, North Africa, Australia
Habitat	Woodland, open country, recently increasing in urban areas
Size	Body: 60–80 centimetres
Status	Least Concern

Tooth
and Claw

GREY WOLF

'Amulet'
by Ted Hughes

Inside the Wolf's fang, the mountain of heather.
Inside the mountain of heather, the Wolf's fur.
Inside the Wolf's fur, the ragged forest.
Inside the ragged forest, the Wolf's foot.
Inside the Wolf's foot, the stony horizon.
Inside the stony horizon, the Wolf's tongue.
Inside the Wolf's tongue, the Doe's tears.
Inside the Doe's tears, the frozen swamp.
Inside the frozen swamp, the Wolf's blood.
Inside the Wolf's blood, the snow wind.
Inside the snow wind, the Wolf's eye.
Inside the Wolf's eye, the North Star.
Inside the North Star, the Wolf's fang.

When a wolf feels threatened, the fur on its back, called its hackles, stands on end. This makes the wolf look bigger and fiercer.

Scientific name   *Canis lupus*
Distribution   North America, Greenland, eastern Europe, Asia
Habitat   Tundra, steppe, open woodland, forest
Size   Body: 1–1.4 metres
Status   Least Concern

LEOPARD SEAL

from *Journals*
by Robert Falcon Scott

One occasionally sees the long lithe sea leopard, formidably armed with ferocious teeth and doubtless containing a penguin or two and perhaps a young crab-eating seal.

This ferocious seal preys mainly on penguins, but it will also eat other kinds of seal. Its mouth is equipped with long, sharp teeth, which are used to cut and tear through flesh.

Scientific name *Hydrurga leptonyx*
Distribution Southern Ocean
Habitat Pack ice, coasts, islands
Size Body: 2.5–3.5 metres
Status Least Concern

Illustrator's note

"To get the drama and action in this painting, I exaggerated the perspective of the seal. Strengthening the colours in the foreground made the main penguin appear to leap out of the page. The air bubbles help to give the impression of movement."

KERMODE BEAR

from *Hunting the Grisly and Other Sketches*
by Theodore Roosevelt

Bears are fond of wallowing in the water, whether in the sand, on the edge of a rapid plains river, on the muddy margin of a pond, or in the oozy moss of a clear, cold mountain spring. One hot August afternoon, as I was clambering down a steep mountain-side near Pend'Oreille lake, I heard a crash some distance below, which showed that a large beast was afoot. On making my way towards the spot, I found I had disturbed a big bear as it was lolling at ease in its bath; the discolored water showed where it had scrambled hastily out and galloped off as I approached. The spring welled out at the base of a high granite rock, forming a small pool of shimmering broken crystal. The soaked moss lay in a deep wet cushion round about, and jutted over the edges of the pool like a floating shelf. Graceful, water-loving ferns swayed to and fro. Above, the great conifers spread their murmuring branches, dimming the light, and keeping out the heat; their brown boles sprang from the ground like buttressed columns. On the barren mountain-side beyond the heat was oppressive. It was small wonder that Bruin should have sought the spot to cool his gross carcass in the fresh spring water.

The bear is a solitary beast, and although many may assemble together, in what looks like a drove, on some favorite feeding-ground – usually where the berries are thick, or by the banks of a salmon-thronged river – the association is never more than momentary, each going its own way as soon as its hunger is satisfied.

The kermode, or spirit, bear has a creamy-white coat and white claws, but is otherwise the same as the American black bear. Kermodes can have black or white cubs, which learn to hunt by watching and copying everything their mother does.

Scientific name *Ursus americanus kermodei*
Distribution Pacific coast of British Colombia, Canada
Habitat Temperate rainforest
Size Body: 1.2–2.2 metres
Status Not evaluated

CHIMPANZEE

from *In the Shadow of Man*
by Jane Goodall

It was October and the short rains had begun. The blackened slopes were softened by feathery new grass shoots and in some places the ground was carpeted by a variety of flowers. The Chimpanzee's spring, I called it. I had had a frustrating morning, tramping up and down three valleys with never a sight or sound of a chimpanzee. Hauling myself up the steep slope of Mlinda Valley I headed for the peak, not only weary but soaking wet from crawling through dense undergrowth. Suddenly I stopped, for I saw a slight movement in the long grass about sixty yards away. Quickly focusing my binoculars I saw that it was a single chimpanzee, and just then he turned in my direction. I recognised David Graybeard.

Cautiously, I moved around so that I could see what he was doing. He was squatting beside the red earth mound of a termite nest, and as I watched I saw him carefully push a long grass stem down into a hole in the mound. After a moment he withdrew it and picked something from the end with his mouth. I was too far away to make out what he was eating, but it was obvious that he was actually using a grass stem as a tool.

I knew that on two occasions casual observers in West Africa had seen chimpanzees using objects as tools: one had broken open palm nut kernels by using a rock as a hammer, and a group of chimps had been observed pushing sticks into an underground bees' nest and licking off the honey. Somehow I had never dreamed of seeing anything so exciting myself.

Chimps cleverly find a meal by inserting sticks into termite mounds. Once the bugs have swarmed over the sticks, the chimps pull them out and eat the termites.

Scientific name	*Pan troglodytes*
Distribution	Africa: Guinea to Democratic Republic of Congo (DRC), Uganda and Tanzania
Habitat	Rainforest, savanna with woodland
Size	Body: 68–94 centimetres
Status	Endangered

LEOPARD

from *International Wildlife Encyclopedia*
by Maurice Burton and Robert Burton

The leopard feeds mainly on small to medium-sized
grazing mammals such as wildebeest, deer and
gazelles, but will eat almost anything that moves.
Prey might range from dung beetles to antelopes
much larger than itself. Commonly it preys upon
impala, steenbok, reedbuck, zebra foals, wildebeest
calves, warthogs and hydraxes. Smaller prey includes
baboons and other monkeys, rodents such as rats
and hares, procupines, ground birds and arthropods.
Small prey is taken more especially by young and
old animals.

Several times it has been found that individual
leopards develop a taste for one particular kind of
prey. One leopard that was studied fed largely on
impala, while another ate only bushpigs and would
travel 2 miles (3 km) each night from its daybed to
hunt these animals. It would seldom molest or take
game closer to home. One well-known leopard of
Lake Kariba in east Africa seemed to eat nothing but
one fish species, in the genus Tilapia. It would lie at
the water's edge until the fish came to the surface
and then catch them with its paw. Another leopard
is said to have developed a preference for frogs.

*Leopards are expert climbers and are incredibly strong. They are
able to drag prey up into trees. Here, they eat undisturbed and
can also keep their leftovers safe from hungry hyenas and jackals.*

Scientific name	*Panthera pardus*
Distribution	Asia: Siberia to Korea, Sri Lanka and Java; middle eastern Africa
Habitat	Desert to forest, lowland plains to mountains
Size	1.3–2.6 metres including tail
Status	Least Concern

FALSE VAMPIRE BAT

from *Concerning Animals and Other Matters*
by E H Aitken

This monster is fond of coming into your bedroom at midnight through the open windows, but not to suck your blood, for it has little in common with the true vampire of South America. It brings its dinner with it and hangs from the ceiling, "feeding like horses when you hear them feed." You hear its jaws working – crunch, crunch, crunch, but feel too drowsy to get up and expel it.

When you get up in the morning there on your clean dressing table, just below the place where it hung, are the bloody remains of a sparrow, or the crumbs of a tree-frog. The servants will tell you that the sparrow was killed and eaten by a rat, but if you rise softly next night when you hear the sound of feeding, and shut the windows, you will find a goblin hanging from the ceiling in the morning, hideous beyond the power of words to tell.

Unlike vampire bats, false vampires do not drink blood. Instead they feed on the flesh of small animals such as frogs, mice, birds and other bats. They have extremely sharp teeth.

Scientific name	*Vampyrum spectrum* (also known as spectrum bat)
Distribution	Mexico to northern South America, Trinidad
Habitat	Tropical forest, rainforest
Size	Body: 13.5–15 centimetres
Status	Near Threatened

AFRICAN ELEPHANT

from *Wild Beasts and Their Ways*
by Sir Samuel W Baker

It feeds heartily, but wastefully, tearing down branches, half of which it leaves untouched; it strips the bark off those trees which it selects as tasteful, but throws wilfully away a considerable portion. Throughout the entire night the elephant is feeding, and it is curious to observe how particular this animal is in the choice of food. Most wild animals possess a certain amount of botanical knowledge which guides them in their grazing; the only exception is the camel, who would poison himself through sheer ignorance and depraved appetite, but the elephant is most careful in its selection of all that is suitable to its requirements. It is astonishing how few of the forest trees are attractive to this animal. Some are tempting from their foliage, others from their bark (vide the powerfully astringent Catechu), some from the succulent roots, and several varieties from the wood, which is eaten like the sugar-cane.

Chewing bark can take an elephant hours, but it is worth it for the extra goodness it contains. Some trees are poisonous, and young elephants learn to avoid these by copying adults in the herd. Bark protects a tree from fungus and insects, so a tree may not survive for long once an elephant has stripped the bark.

Scientific name   *Loxodonta africana*
Distribution   Africa, south of the Sahara Desert
Habitat   Forest, savanna, grassland
Size   Body: 6–7.5 metres
Status   Vulnerable

Illustrator's note
"The technicality of the detail in the wrinkles of the skin involves careful working on the highlights and shadows. Each wrinkle needs to be meticulously defined and takes a lot of time and concentration."

NILE CROCODILE

from *Travels in the Interior Districts of Africa*
by Mungo Park

On the 4th they agreed with the canoe people for sixty bars, to transport the cattle and baggage across the river, and as there was but a single canoe, the day was far spent before the business could be accomplished. Isaaco exerted himself very much in pushing the asses into the water, and shoving along the canoe; but being apprehensive that the whole could not be conveyed over in the course of the day, he went farther down, attempting to drive six asses across at once, where the water was not so deep.

About the middle of the river, a crocodile rose up close to him, laying hold of his left thigh, and pulling him under water. With the most astonishing presence of mind he groped for the animal's head, thrusting his finger into its eye, the pain of which forced it to let go its hold. The crocodile returned, and seized him by the other thigh, pulling him under water, as he had done before, and Isaaco thrust his fingers into its eyes with so much violence, that it again quitted its hold, rose to the surface, and tumbled about as in a state of stupidity. When Mr. Park got over, he found poor Isaaco very much lacerated in both his thighs. The wound on the left thigh was four inches long, the other not quite so large, but very deep. Our traveller drew the lips of the wounds together with pieces of adhesive plaster, secured by means of rollers, and being at no great distance from a village, he judged it prudent to go on before his wounds became painful.

To catch its prey, the Nile crocodile lies very still in the water. When the prey comes close, the crocodile shoots out of its hiding place to catch the animal in its powerful jaws. These huge reptiles feed on fish, birds, antelopes, zebras and even buffaloes.

Scientific name	*Crocodylus niloticus*
Distribution	Africa, western Madagascar
Habitat	Large rivers, lakes, marshes
Size	4.5–5 metres including tail
Status	Least Concern

Fight or Flight

BROWN BEAR

from 'The Female of the Species'
by Rudyard Kipling

When the Himalayan peasant meets the he-bear in his pride,
He shouts to scare the monster who will often turn aside.
But the she-bear thus accosted rends the peasant tooth and nail,
For the female of the species is more deadly than the male.

*Brown bears are generally solitary animals, but they may gather in groups
in an area where food is abundant. This can lead to fighting between males,
which lash out with their powerful paws, jaws and claws.*

Scientific name   *Ursus arctos*
Distribution   Northern Europe, Siberia, Asia,
Alaska, Canada, mountainous
areas of western USA
Habitat   Forest, tundra
Size   Body: 1.5–2.5 metres
Status   Least Concern

CAMARGUE

from *White Horses over France*
by Robin Hanbury-Tenison

If you read some of the lavishly illustrated guide books to the Camargue, you will learn that the white horses of the region are the scarcely modified descendants of the original wild horses which populated prehistoric Gaul and are reproduced in cave painting at Lascaux… it would be nice to think that these romantic herds of wild horses have lived in the same desolate region of France, breeding pure for thousands of years. Certainly there have been famous horses there for a long time. There is a letter dated AD 399 from the prefect of Rome to a friend of his farming in the Camargue asking him to supply some sturdy steeds to be raced in one of the circuses… they have lived for an exceptionally long time in the wetlands of the Rhône delta and they have adapted in remarkable ways to the harsh conditions to be found there, becoming exceptionally hardy and resilient. They have been bred selectively for their intelligence and skill at working with cattle and coping with difficult and dangerous terrain. Best of all, they are recognized as having exceptionally nice natures so that they will respond to their names being called at a great distance and approach their masters.

Camargues live in wild herds. They are very strong, and are well-suited to living in wet, marshy areas. Broad hooves help them gallop across wetlands or through the sea.

Scientific name	*Equus caballus*
Distribution	Camargue region of the Rhône delta in France
Habitat	Grassland
Size	1.42 metres to the shoulder
Status	Least Concern

LESSER BUSHBABY

from *The Bafut Beagles*
by Gerald Durrell

It came drifting through the tangled branches with all the gentle, airy grace of a piece of thistledown. When it got nearer, I discovered that it looked exactly like my idea of a leprechaun: it was clad in a little coat of greenish-grey and it had a long, slender, furry tail. Its hands, which were pink, were large for its size, and its fingers were tremendously long and attenuated. Its ears were large and the skin so fine that it was semi-transparent; these ears seemed to have a life of their own, for they twisted and turned independently, sometimes crumpling and folding flat to the head as if they were a fan, at others standing up pricked and straight like anaemic arum lilies. The face of the little creature was dominated by a pair of tremendous dark eyes, eyes that would put any self-respecting owl to shame. Moreover, the creature could twist its head and look over its back in much the same way that an owl does. It ran to the tip of a slender branch that scarcely dipped beneath its weight and there it sat, clutching the bark with its long slender fingers, peering about with its great eyes and chirruping dimly to itself. It was, I knew, a galago but it looked much more like something out of a fairy tale.

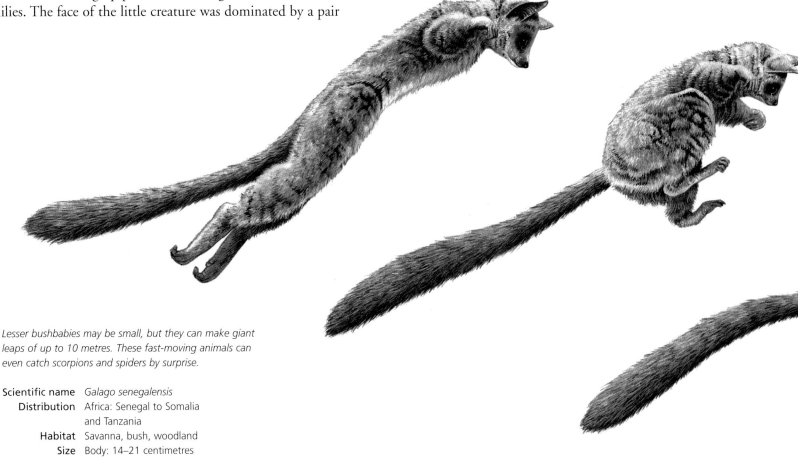

Lesser bushbabies may be small, but they can make giant leaps of up to 10 metres. These fast-moving animals can even catch scorpions and spiders by surprise.

Scientific name	*Galago senegalensis*
Distribution	Africa: Senegal to Somalia and Tanzania
Habitat	Savanna, bush, woodland
Size	Body: 14–21 centimetres
Status	Least Concern

SPINY PUFFER FISH

'Puffer Fish'
by Max Fatchen

A puffer fish blows up with air
And some may think this crafty
It blows and blows,
And so it grows
But goodness me, how draughty.

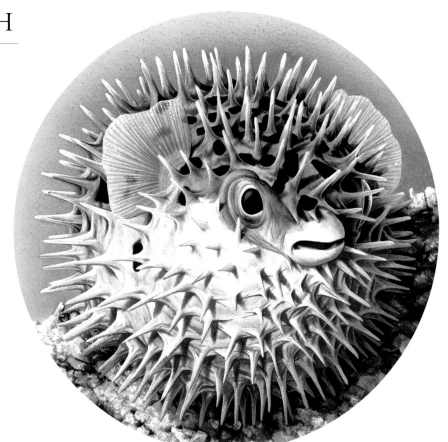

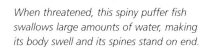

When threatened, this spiny puffer fish swallows large amounts of water, making its body swell and its spines stand on end.

Scientific name	*Diodon holacanthus*
Distribution	Warm ocean waters, Caribbean and Red Sea
Habitat	Shallow, coastal regions
Size	30–60 centimetres
Status	Least Concern

CHEETAH

from *Life on Earth*
by Sir David Attenborough

In order to catch the grazers, the predators of the plain have to improve greatly their running technique. They have not taken to moving on the tips of a reduced number of toes perhaps because they have always needed their toes, armed with claws, as offensive weapons. Their solution is different. They have effectively lengthened their limbs by making their spine extremely flexible. At full stretch, travelling at high speed, their hind and front legs overlap one another beneath the body just like those of a galloping antelope. The cheetah has a thin elongated body and is said to be the fastest animal on earth, capable of reaching speeds, in bursts, of over 110 kph. But this method is very energy-consuming. Great muscular effort is needed to keep the spine springing back and forth and the cheetah cannot maintain such speeds for more than a minute or so. Either it succeeds in outrunning its prey within a few hundred yards and makes a kill or it has to retire exhausted while the antelope, with their more rigid backs and long lever-legs, continue to gallop off to a safer part of the plains.

The cheetah is the fastest animal on land. It prefers wide open spaces where it can easily spot prey, such as gazelles. The cheetah remains hidden from view until it's close enough to its prey to give a short, rapid chase.

Scientific name	*Acinonyx jubatus*
Distribution	Africa, east to Asia: eastern Iran
Habitat	Open country, desert, savanna
Size	1.8–2.1 metres including tail
Status	Vulnerable

LAR GIBBON

from *Green Mansions*
by W H Hudson

Thus in idleness, with such thoughts for company, I spent my time, glad that no human being, savage or civilized, was with me. It was better to be alone to listen to the monkeys that chattered without offending; to watch them occupied with the unserious business of their lives. With that luxuriant tropical nature, its green clouds and illusive aerial spaces, full of mystery, they harmonized well in language, appearance, and motions – mountebank angels, living their fantastic lives far above earth in a half-way heaven of their own.

Gibbons make death-defying leaps between trees, covering up to 15 metres at a time, at great speed. The swinging movement is called brachiation, and it allows gibbons to reach speeds of up to 56 kilometres an hour.

Scientific name	*Hylobates lar*
Distribution	Southeast Asia including China, Thailand, Laos, Burma, Malay Peninsula and Sumatra
Habitat	Rainforest, dry forest
Size	Body: 42–58 centimetres
Status	Near Threatened

Illustrator's note

"The execution of this painting involved careful study of the way fur lies, often separating in clumps and partings. The four studies show the way the animal swings through the trees illustrating the flow of its silky fur."

BROWN LONG-EARED BAT

A poem by Emily Dickinson

The bat is dun with wrinkled wings
    Like fallow article,
And not a song pervades his lips,
    Or none perceptible.

His small umbrella, quaintly halved,
    Describing in the air
An arc alike inscrutable, –
    Elate philosopher!

Deputed from what firmament
    Of what astute abode,
Empowered with what malevolence
    Auspiciously withheld.

To his adroit Creator
    Ascribe no less the praise;
Beneficent, believe me,
    His eccentricities.

Brown long-eared bats live on a diet of insects. Their hearing is so good that they can detect the movement of a single insect on the ground.

Scientific name   *Plecotus auritus*
Distribution   Europe, Central Asia
Habitat   Sheltered, lightly wooded areas
Size   Body: 4–5 centimetres
Status   Least Concern

PIPISTRELLE BAT

from *Fables*
by Aesop

A great conflict was about to come off between the Birds and the Beasts. When the two armies were collected together the Bat hesitated which to join. The Birds that passed his perch said: "Come with us"; but he said: "I am a Beast." Later on, some Beasts who were passing underneath him looked up and said: "Come with us"; but he said: "I am a Bird." Luckily at the last moment peace was made, and no battle took place, so the Bat came to the Birds and wished to join in the rejoicings, but they all turned against him and he had to fly away. He then went to the Beasts, but soon had to beat a retreat, or else they would have torn him to pieces. "Ah," said the Bat, "I see now, He that is neither one thing nor the other has no friends."

These small creatures are perhaps the commonest European bats. They are unlikely to be spotted in winter, but during summer they swoop and dive, with a characteristic jerky flight.

Scientific name	*Pipistrellus pipistrellus*
Distribution	Europe and eastwards to China
Habitat	Forest, urban areas, open land
Size	Body: 3–4.5 centimetres
Status	Least Concern

SERVAL

from *The Life of Mammals*
by Sir David Attenborough

The serval, a small species with particularly long legs bounces its way through tall grass pursuing mice and rats. So skilled is it at pouncing and so gymnastic in doing so that it can suddenly switch its attention away from little rodents scurrying ahead of it through the grass and bring down a low-flying bird with a swat of its forepaw.

Servals have long legs and a long neck. This enables them to see and hear clearly in long grass. They are excellent pouncers and leap to strike their prey with their forepaws.

Scientific name	*Leptailurus serval*
Distribution	Africa, south of the Sahara Desert to South Africa
Habitat	Savanna, open plains, woodland
Size	0.9–1.35 metres including tail
Status	Least Concern

HIPPOPOTAMUS

from *An Account of Egypt*
by Herodotus

The river-horse is sacred in the district of Papremis, but for the other Egyptians he is not sacred; and this is the appearance which he presents: he is four-footed, cloven-hoofed like an ox, flat-nosed, with a mane like a horse and showing teeth like tusks, with a tail and voice like a horse and in size as large as the largest ox; and his hide is so exceedingly thick that when it has been dried shafts of javelins are made of it.

Male hippos are highly territorial. They will roar at each other and, if neither gives way, they will fight using their massive teeth as weapons. A battle may last for hours and severe injuries can occur, leading to the death of at least one hippo.

Scientific name	*Hippopotamus amphibius*
Distribution	Africa, south of the Sahara Desert to Namibia and South Africa
Habitat	Rivers or lakes in grassland
Size	Body: 3.5–5 metres
Status	Vulnerable

Illustrator's note

"I captured the play of light on the wet hides using lots of reflective light. The heavy use of dark shadows and the dramatic splashing of water help to bring out the character of these ungainly animals."

Author biographies

Aesop

620–560 BC
Greek slave and writer

Very little is known about Aesop's life, but it is believed he was a slave and tradition says he was also exceptionally ugly. Plato, the great philosopher, admired his works.

Aitken, E H

1851–1909
English civil servant

An employee of the British government in India by profession, Aitken pursued his hobby of studying wildlife in his spare time and writing delightful books such as *A Naturalist on the Prowl* and *Behind the Bungalow*.

Amundsen, Roald

1872–1928
Norwegian polar explorer

The first successful Antarctic expedition to the South Pole was led by Amundsen and he was the first person to reach both the North and South Poles. He also succeeded in traversing the Northwest Passage, something explorers had been trying to do since the days of Christopher Columbus. He disappeared in June 1928 while taking part in a rescue mission.

Attenborough, Sir David

Born 1926
English naturalist and broadcaster

For more than 50 years, Sir David Attenborough has been making his hugely popular wildlife programmes for the BBC. His latest documentary series, *Life in Cold Blood*, explores the lives of reptiles and amphibians and was broadcast in 2008. It has been said that Attenborough is probably the most widely travelled man on the planet.

Baker, Olaf

1876–1964
Anglo-American writer

Born in England in the 1870s, Olaf Baker migrated to the United States in 1902 where he wrote *Shasta of the Wolves* and *Where the Buffaloes Begin*, among other works.

Baker, Sir Samuel W

1821–1893
English explorer

A flamboyant character, White bought his second wife at a slave auction in Bulgaria in 1859. She accompanied him on his dangerous African expedition in his attempt to trace the source of the river Nile.

Benson, A C

1862–1925
English essayist, poet and author

Benson was the son of the Archbishop of Canterbury, one of six children, none of whom ever married. He was Master of a Cambridge college and wrote the words for one of Britain's most famous patriotic songs, Land of Hope and Glory. His diary, published after his death, was one of the longest ever written, at four million words.

Bierce, Ambrose

1842–1914
American journalist and writer

One of 13 siblings, Bierce lived a life of wild adventure. He fought in the Civil War, searched for gold, wrote vicious pieces of journalism and a brilliantly witty book, *The Devil's Dictionary*. He disappeared without trace in Mexico.

Burroughs, John

1837–1921
American naturalist and essayist

Speaking of the view from the highest mountain in his native Catskill range, John Burroughs once said: "The works of man dwindle, and the original features of the huge globe come out. Every single object or point is dwarfed; the valley of the Hudson is only a wrinkle in the earth's surface. You discover with a feeling of surprise that the great thing is the earth itself..."

Burton, Maurice

1898–1992
English zoologist

Dr Maurice Burton was the sponge specialist at the Natural History museum in London and became its deputy director of Zoology. He retired to write popular naturalist books for children.

Cherry-Garrard, Apsley

1886–1959
English explorer

A support member of the doomed Scott Polar expedition, Apsley Cherry-Garrard made the trek to find the bodies of Scott and his companions. He was nicknamed 'Cheery' by his companions and wrote of the expedition: 'We kept our tempers – even with God.'

Clapham, Richard

1878–1954
English author

Clapham grew up in a historic country house, Austwick Hall, in the Yorkshire dales. He wrote many books on hunting, fishing and shooting, which also celebrated the animals under pursuit.

Darwin, Charles

1809–1882
English naturalist

A poor student, Darwin became one of the greatest scientists of all time when he formulated his theory of evolution, following a five-year trip on the *Beagle* as the ship's naturalist.

Dickinson, Emily

1830–1886
American poet

An shy, reclusive woman, Dickinson almost always wore white and she rarely travelled outside her town of Amherst, Massachusetts. Only a handful of her poems were published in her lifetime.

Dovaston, John F M

1782–1854
English landowner and writer

After a brief career as a theatre critic, Dovaston inherited his father's estate in

Shropshire where he settled down to life as an amateur musician and keen naturalist. He rose at five every morning and died a bachelor. He held a long correspondence with Thomas Bewick, famous for his drawings of birds.

Durrell, Gerald

1925–1995
English naturalist, conservationist, zookeeper and author

A larger-than-life figure in every sense, Durrell wrote wonderfully funny books about his travels to collect animals for his breeding zoo on the island of Jersey. His most famous book was *My Family and Other Animals*, which was published in 1956. Durrell's main concern always centred on the conservation of rare animal species.

Dybek, Stuart

Born 1942
American writer

Dybek is a Professor of English and writes novels and poems. He has been recognized as one of America's foremost writers of short stories.

Fabre, Jean-Henri

1823–1915
French entomologist and writer

A self-taught writer of approachable books about insects, Fabre wrote of his critics: "They fear lest a page that is read without fatigue should not always be the expression of the truth. Were I to take their word for it, we are profound only on condition of being obscure."

Fatchen, Max

Born 1920
Australian journalist, poet and writer

Max Fatchen was born on a remote Australian farm and studied at home, only travelling, by horse and cart, to school once a week to get his homework marked. He lists his hobbies as fishing and talking to children.

Fiser, Karen

Born 1945
American poet

Karen Fiser began writing poems during a long struggle with disability and chronic pain. Her first book of poems, *Words Like Fate and Pain*, was published in 1992.

Fleming, Marjorie

1803–1811
Scottish diarist and poet

Although she died of meningitis, following measles, aged just eight years old, Marjorie Fleming is still remembered for the diary she wrote in the last 18 months of her life, and for her delightful, lively poems.

Frost, Robert

1874–1963
American poet

A much-loved writer of poems such as 'The Road Not Taken' and 'Mending Wall', Frost's work celebrates the rural landscape and life of New England. He taught English in many colleges and encouraged his students to find the human voice in their own writing. His epitaph reads: 'I had a lover's quarrel with the world'.

Fry, Stephen

Born 1957
English humourist, writer, TV presenter and actor

A much-loved English television figure, Stephen Fry drives a black London taxi, and is passionately devoted to computers (he bought the second Macintosh sold in the UK). His comedy partner is Hugh Laurie, and he is godfather to all three of Laurie's children.

Goldsmith, Oliver

c.1730–1774
Irish playwright and author

As an adult, Goldsmith lived in London, where a friend described him as an inspired idiot because of his talented writing, gambling addiction, and disorganized life (he failed to emigrate to America because he missed the boat).

Goodall, Jane

Born 1934
English primatologist and ethnologist

Famous for her 45-year-long study of chimpanzees, Goodall's interest in the animals began as a child when her father gave her a stuffed toy chimpanzee, which still sits on her dresser today.

Grahame, Kenneth

1859–1932
English bank official and writer

Grahame led a sad life, but wrote one of the most idyllic and best-loved children's books, *The Wind in the Willows*. His epitaph reads: 'To the beautiful memory of Kenneth Grahame, husband of Elspeth and father of Alastair, who passed the River on the 6 July 1932, leaving childhood and literature through him the more blest for all time'.

Hanbury-Tenison, Robin

Born 1936
English explorer, conservationist and author

Hanbury-Tenison has been on more than 30 expeditions and is the founder of Survival International, a charity to help tribal people of the world. In 1982 he was named by the *Sunday Times* as the greatest explorer of the past 20 years.

Herodotus

c. 484–425 BC
Greek historian

Living in Harlicarnassus in what is now Turkey, Herodotus was the first historian to collect materials systematically, test their accuracy to some degree and arrange them into a well-told narrative.

Hudson, W H

1841–1922
Anglo-American writer

Born in Argentina, Hudson loved the wild, open spaces. Moving to England, he became an expert on ornithology and wrote many books on the subject.

Hughes, Ted

1930–1998
English poet and children's author

Much of Ted Hughes' poetry is rooted in nature, and in the innocent savagery and beauty of animals. He was Poet Laureate from 1984 until his death and also wrote the children's classic *The Iron Man*.

Jennings, Elizabeth

1926–2001
English poet

Born in Lincolnshire, in the east of England, Jennings moved to Oxfordshire when she was six and spent the remainder of her life there, briefly working as a librarian but mostly writing her clear, beautiful poetry.

Kingsley, Charles

1819–1875
English novelist

Kingsley was an extremely passionate social reformer. *The Water Babies*, his most famous novel, played a major part in ending the dangerous practice of sending small boys up chimneys to clean them.

Kipling, Rudyard

1865–1936
English writer of poems, short stories, and novels

Among Kipling's many publications are the *Jungle Books*, *Just So Stories* and *Kim*, a tale of a boy in India. Kipling is the youngest ever recipient of the Nobel prize for literature.

Lawrence, D H

1885–1930
English poet and novelist

Now recognized as one of the great modern authors, Lawrence's work was seen as shocking in its day. He died aged 44, from tuberculosis.

Longfellow, Henry Wadsworth

1807–1882
American poet and professor

Longfellow was a distinguished poet, and was much loved for his narrative poems such as 'The Ride of Paul Revere' and 'Hiawatha'.

Lydekker, Richard

1849–1915
English naturalist, geologist and writer

Well known as a writer on natural history subjects, Lydekker is responsible for the ten-volume catalogue of fossils that is held in the Natural History Museum in London.

Martel, Yann

Born 1963
Canadian author

Born in Spain, Yann grew up in Alaska, British Columbia, Costa Rica, France, Ontario and Mexico, and has continued travelling as an adult, spending time in Iran, Turkey and India. His most famous book is *Life of Pi*, the story of a boy adrift in a small boat with a tiger.

Matthiessen, Peter

Born 1927
American naturalist, author and explorer

As well as travelling extensively throughout some of the greatest wildernesses known to man, Matthiessen has also written widely about those peoples who live in such places, particularly of the American Indian. Matthiessen was the official State Author of New York 1995–1997. He practises Zen Buddhism and is a Buddhist priest.

Melville, Herman

1819–1891
American poet and novelist

Melville's most famous work, *Moby-Dick* is now seen as one of the greatest novels of world literature. However, in his time it was regarded as a failure – the initial 3000 print run failed to sell out during Melville's lifetime. Born in New York, Melville wrote from personal experience, having started his sailing career as a cabin boy on a ship to Liverpool.

Morris, Francis Orpen

1810–1893
English clergyman

From his Yorkshire parish, Morris wrote scholarly books on birds, moths and butterflies, as well as children's books. He was bad-tempered, loathed feminism, and he was also a fierce opponent of Charles Darwin.

Park, Mungo

1771–1806
Scottish explorer and doctor

A prolific but unfortunate explorer, Park led two expeditions to Africa to determine the course of the Niger River. He and his fellow explorers died on the second trip when his boat was attacked by hostile natives.

Polisar, Barry Louis

Born 1954
American songwriter and author

Poet and lyricist, Barry has written songs for *Sesame Street* and has been entertaining children for over 30 years. Most recently his music featured in the hit film *Juno*.

Post, Laurens van der

1906–1996
South African writer

Laurens van der Post loved his native Africa deeply and wrote movingly about its landscape and people. He was godfather to Prince William and a friend of Prince Charles.

Readicker-Henderson, Ed and Lynn

American travel writers

Ed and Lynn are a husband and wife team of travel writers who have lived in Alaska for over 15 years. They think they have seen just about everything there is to see in that vast state.

Rees, Alfred W

1872–1917
Naturalist

Alfred Rees was well-respected as an expert in the fields of ornithology and entomology, and lived in Wales.

Richmond, Simon

Born 1965
English writer and photographer

Richmond specializes in writing about food and travel and has written over 30 guide books. He has lived for several years in Japan and now divides his time between the US and Australia.

Roosevelt, Theodore

1858–1919
26th president of the United States

Roosevelt's lifelong interest in animals was formed when, aged seven, he saw a dead seal at a market. After obtaining the seal's head, the young Roosevelt and two of his cousins started collecting and stuffing animals for their own museum of natural history.

Scott, Robert Falcon

1868–1912
English Royal Naval officer and explorer

Scott was leader of the doomed 1912 expedition to the South Pole. The five-man team reached the pole to find it had already been claimed by Amundsen some five weeks earlier. All five men died on the return 800-mile journey.

Serraillier, Ian

1912–1994
English novelist and poet

Ian Serraillier wrote delightful poetry and retellings of famous stories. However, he is best known for his masterpiece *The Silver Sword*, which tells the story of a family of child refugees seeking their parents in the chaos that followed the end of World War II.

Warren, Lynne

American journalist

A journalist working on the *National Geographic* magazine, Warren says she loves the amazing things that words can do, and believes that writing needs to be as true as it can be.

Weddell, James

1787–1834
English sailor and explorer

In 1823, as captain aboard the sealing ship *Jane*, Weddell travelled further south than anyone had been before, a record that held for more than 80 years. He wrote several books about his voyages and a breed of seal is named after him.

White, Gilbert

1720–1793
English clergyman and naturalist

White is regarded by many as the first ecologist. Unlike his contemporaries, he studied nature in the field, rather than from stuffed specimens, and wrote letters to a famous biologist about what he found. Many of his observations also involve his pet tortoise, Timothy.

White, T H

1906–1964
English writer

White's best-known book is *The Sword in the Stone*, the story of the boyhood of King Arthur. It was identified by J K Rowling as a major influence on her writing, and she described the hero as Harry Potter's spiritual ancestor.

Wood, John George

1827–1889
English clergyman and naturalist.

He was the author of popular books on nature, whose *Common Objects of the Country* sold 100,000 in one week when it was published.

Youatt, William

1776–1847
English vet and writer

William Youatt was a much-respected scientific writer on animals, and an acknowledged expert on cattle, small animals and horses.

Sources

Chambers Encyclopedia

1859
Scottish fount of knowledge

The *Chambers Encyclopedia* was founded by two brothers, William and Robert Chambers. Their family was ruined in the Napoleonic wars and they were forced to find work in order to help their family. Starting as booksellers, they gradually came to write and print their own books and journals on subjects such as science, maths, geography and literature. Out of this grew their project for the *Chambers Encyclopedia*, one of the most popular and bestselling encyclopedias in the world. Both brothers were born with six fingers on each hand and six toes on each foot.

Wikipedia, The Free Encyclopedia

2001
American and international online encyclopedia

Wikipedia is the fastest-growing, largest and most popular general reference work on the Internet. It has over 10 million articles and is visited by nearly 700 million people a year.

Index

Acknowledgements

Page 10, 17, 35, 74, 112, 118 Reproduced with kind permission from Sir David Attenborough.

11 From 'The Deer's Request', published in *Collected Poems* by Carcanet. Reproduced with permission from David Higham Associates.

14 From 'Inspiration', published in *TriQuarterly* Magazine. Reproduced with permission from the author Stuart Dybek.

18 From *Life of Pi* by Yann Martel, first published in Great Britain by Canongate Books Ltd, 14 High Street, Edinburgh, EH1 1TE. From *Life of Pi*. (Canongate Books Ltd., 2002/Alfred A. Knopf Canada, 2001) © 2001 by Yann Martel. With permission of the author.

24 © Estate of Ian Serraillier.

37 'The Bear' from *The Poetry of Robert Frost* edited by Edward Connery Lathem, published by Jonathan Cape. Reprinted by permission of The Random House Group Ltd. Excerpt from 'The Bear' from *The Poetry of Robert Frost* edited by Edward Connery Lathem. Copyright 1928, 1969 by Henry Holt and Company. Copyright 1956 by Robert Frost. Reprinted by permission of Henry Holt and Company, LLC.

38 From *Losing and Finding*, by Karen Fiser (Denton: University of North Texas Press, 2003). Copyright 2003 by Karen Fiser, reprinted by permission of the publisher.

40(l) Reproduced with permission from Ayer Company Publishers.

42, 43, 89, 110 Reproduced with permission of Curtis Brown Group Ltd, London on behalf of the Estate of Gerald Durrell Copyright © Gerald Durrell 1954, 1991.

56 Reproduced with permission from Hunter Publishing Inc.

57 *Wikipedia, The Free Encyclopedia*.

58 From *The Snow Leopard* by Peter Matthiessen, published by Chatto & Windus. Reprinted by permission of The Random House group Ltd.

66 'Emperor Penguins' © 1993 by Barry Louis Polisar from the book *Peculiar Zoo* Published by Rainbow Morning Music, USA.

68 Published by Putnams. Reproduced with permission from David Higham Associates.

69 Reproduced with permission from *Malaysia, Singapore and Brunei, 10th Edition* © 2007 Lonely Planet Publications.

83 Published by Hutchinson. Reproduced with permission from David Higham Associates.

84 Lynne Warren/National Geographic Image Collection.

86 From *The Heart of the Hunter* by Laurens van der Post. Published by Vintage, £7.99.

93 'Amulet' from *Moon-bells and Other Poems* by Ted Hughes. Reproduced with permission from Faber and Faber Ltd.

98 Excerpt from *In the Shadow of Man* by Jane Goodall. Copyright © 1971 by Hugo and Jane van Lawick-Goodall. Reprinted by permission of Houghton Mifflin Harcourt Publishing Company. All rights reserved.

100 From *International Wildlife Encyclopedia*. Reproduced with permission from Marshall Cavendish Corporation, New York © 2002.

108 *White Horses over France* By Robin Hanbury-Tenison (© Robin Hanbury-Tenison) is reproduced by permission of PFD (www.pfd.co.uk) on behalf of Robin Hanbury-Tenison.

111 'Puffer Fish' from *Songs for My Dog and Other Wry Rhymes* by Max Fatchen (Wakefield Press, 1999).

The publishers have made every effort to contact all copyright holders, but apologize if any source remains unacknowledged.

First published in 2008 by Miles Kelly Publishing Ltd, Bardfield Centre, Great Bardfield, Essex, CM7 4SL

Copyright © Miles Kelly Publishing Ltd 2008

10 9 8 7 6 5 4 3 2 1

Editorial Director Belinda Gallagher

Art Director Jo Brewer

Editorial Assistant Sarah Parkin

Compiler Tig Thomas

Consultant Camilla de la Bedoyere

Cover Designer Jo Brewer

Design Concept Rachel Cross

Designer Joe Jones

Production Manager Elizabeth Brunwin

Reprographics Stephan Davis, Ian Paulyn

ISBN 978-1-84810-054-1

Printed in China

British Library Cataloguing-in-Publication Data
A catalogue record for this book is available from the British Library

Made with paper from a sustainable forest

www.mileskelly.net
info@mileskelly.net

www.factsforprojects.com

Conservation Status

The World Conservation Union (IUCN) produces a Red List of threatened species of animals and plants. The Red List uses categories to describe the degree of threat, and the following categories appear in this book.

Threatened

Critically Endangered (CR): Species has an extremely high risk of becoming extinct in the wild in the immediate future.

Endangered (EN): Species has a very high risk of becoming extinct in the wild in the near future.

Vulnerable (VU): Species is not critically endangered, or endangered, but faces a high risk of extinction in the wild in the medium-term future.

Lower risk

Near Threatened (NT): Species is close to becoming Vulnerable.

Least Concern (LC): Species has been evaluated but does not qualify for any other category.

Not evaluated: The conservation status of this species has not been assessed.